SHORTCUT TO FLOW

The Step-by-Step Process for Achieving Extraordinary Focused Success

Anders Piper

Copyright © 2011 Anders Piper

All rights reserved.

ISBN-13: 978-87-992469-1-5
ISBN-13:978-1461061274
ISBN-10:146106127X

DEDICATION

This book is dedicated to Mihaly Csikszentmihalyi for his great work on Flow and all to the Masters who have taught me my wisdom including the amazing Dr. Richard Bandler who has been so generous in providing me the opportunity to acquire unique knowledge and skills and John and Kathleen La Valle for having shared so much of their wisdom and humor. Also a special thanks to Elvis Lester who has been an inspiration and mentor to me for a long time and, finally to my wife Anne and my two children Hannah and Emil for accepting all my absence and travels in the pursuit of knowledge, wisdom and experience.

CONTENTS

	Forward by Dr. Richard Bandler	Pg 6
	Acknowledgments	Pg 7
	A Word from the Editor, Elvis Lester	Pg 8
1	Introduction	Pg 9
2	The Dream	Pg 11
3	Happiness and all that Jazz	Pg 17
4	Perception	Pg 23
5	Flow and the Structure of Thinking	Pg 29
6	The Formula for Flow	Pg 45
7	Using Mental Training to Promote Flow	Pg 50
8	I Have a Dream	Pg 56
9	Well Formed Outcomes	Pg 63
10	Compelling Visions for your Directions	Pg 71
11	Feedback	Pg 80
12	Stay Focused	Pg 87
13	Skills	Pg 95
14	Get the State	Pg 103
15	The Not so Flow Scenarios	Pg 109
16	The Art of Flow	Pg 114
17	About the Author	Pg 125
18	Resources	Pg 126
19	Bibliography	Pg 127

FORWARD

I am pleased to write an introduction for Anders Pipers book. He has studied with me for many years, and has been a great student, and a great teacher of NLP. This work places practical tools in the hands of those who wish to be more successful.

I believe there is a great need for more NLP skills to find their way into the hands of the business community. This book fills at least part of that bill. What Anders has done here is just what all great NLP is about, taking the complex nature of success and making it simple to learn.

In this book he will teach you a lot about the power of being focused. Fulfilling your dreams is a big challenge for all of us. Having a clear focus on what they are, and the tools to achieve the right mental conditioning to achieve them will help you get there.

I highly recommend that you read this book and master the ART OF THE FLOW!!!!

Dr. Richard Bandler
co-creator of NLP

ACKNOWLEDGMENTS

The content in this book is based upon the concept of Flow developed by Mihaly Csikszentmihalyi. The methods and techniques for helping you get into Flow are based on Neuro-Linguistic Programming created by Dr. Richard Bandler and John Grinder. There are some of the techniques that are created by one of their early students Robert Dilts and there is one technique developed by my close friend Elvis Lester, who also has been so kind and generous as to edit this book. I would also like to thank Shelle Rose Charvet for letting me use her definitions of the LAB Profile.

As NLP is a developing field there may be others who have been involved in generating these methods, models and techniques and they shall hereby be given due credit, but no one has contributed so much to field of NLP and its development as Dr. Richard Bandler and I invite all to acknowledge his immortal contributions to the field of NLP and human wellbeing.

A WORD FROM ELVIS LESTER, THE EDITOR OF THIS BOOK

When you delve into this book you will find powerful ways to "design engineer" flow into your experiences and into your life. Anders Piper has invested much time and energy into the study, practice and perfection of his art. He has worked with world-renowned masters of human performance improvement gathering knowledge of how to accelerate human performance and put it to the test.

Shortcut to Flow reveals to you some of the secrets he has learned along this journey to creating flow by design with more intention. It is made clear in this work that through devotion to your craft, commitment and discipline to "running your own brain" with more ease and elegance you will enhance your ability to achieve the oft sought after "state of happiness and satisfaction" which comes as a result of focusing your attention upon what matters most to you and absorbing yourself into your work and your art simply for the sake of doing.

Here, Anders provides you the reader the opportunity to lift the veil and look directly into how you can "start from flow", and take advantage and do what you love most, attain happiness as a natural by-product of your efforts and exceed your wildest dreams. Get this book and devour it, integrate it into your very treasure trove of tools and technics that will transform your life.

Elvis Lester, MA, Sr. LMHC, NCC, MAC, NBCFCH
Licensed Mental Health Counselor (State of FL)
Licensed Master Trainer of NLP & Hypnosis

I INTRODUCTION

Through more than 25 years Mihaly Csikszentmihalyi has been researching the concept of Flow and he has published several great books about the subject. This book is based on his theory on Flow and very much inspired by his works.

This book is not meant to be a redefinition of the term Flow, but rather an attempt of making it tangible. Mihaly has better than anybody described the term Flow and it would be an insult to his great work to try to alter this. This book is for those who have a desire to experience Flow either for themselves more often – or for those who are leaders or coaches and have the need to help other people into Flow.

Apart from the theory of Mihaly Csikszentmihalyi, this book consists of knowledge from the field of general psychology and NLP (Neuro-Linguistic Programming). No other field offers so many tangible techniques that can make theoretical concepts come alive as NLP.

Although not directly a part of Flow, we will also touch upon Thinking Structures/Meta Programs and have a closer look at how they can either support or prevent Flow from happening. Some Meta Programs seem to promote the state of Flow and some don't.

What started out as little notes on a napkin in a restaurant in Helsinki became the background material for this book and for this I would like to thank Arne Maus from Germany for his help and support in creating the foundation for this book. His many years of work with Thinking Structures (Meta Programs) and Motivation with the help of Professor Dr. David Scheffer from the Nord Akademie in Northern Germany has been of great inspiration. No other tool can support the work with Flow as well as the Identity Compass Profile which measures directly if people are within the motivational states to generate Flow.

This book is not an attempt to make Flow complicated – on the contrary – this is an attempt at helping as many as possible to direct them into the wonderful feeling of Flow.

If you have trained NLP techniques before, you may very well know some of the techniques in this book. What I offer is the sequence and combination of techniques that will send you in the right direction.

I wish you lots of fun.

Anders Piper
M.Sc. Psych and Licensed NLP Master Trainer

2 THE DREAM

He looked up and realized that he was getting close to the top. In his head he had the route imprinted and he knew that now all that was left was exactly 6 more serpentine turns and coming out of the last turn there would be 400 meters to the finish line.

It had been a cruel day, hot as hell and long and sweat was pouring from him. He had been under pressure from his competitors right from the start, where a bunch of young riders early on had taken off in pursuit of television fame and had taken one of his worst competitors with them.

Today's stage with a total of 197 km had more altitude meters than any previous stage and there was no doubt that it would separate the serious contenders from the rest of the group.

He monitored his legs and his body, sensed every muscle, noted the condition they were in and then he smiled, probably more on the inside than on the outside. But there was a smile on his lips and for the spectators he passed at that moment, it must have looked awesome, for a man in his condition under these conditions to smile. He'd just had a glance over his shoulders and what he saw was faces in agony, torn and twisted and although staying right on his rear wheel, he sensed despair in their faces and he liked it.

From the many lonely training rides he knew every meter of the asphalt on these last kilometers. He knew every flower on the roadside which he had monitored through the season and now, where all the flowers were squashed under the feet of the masses hysterically dancing on the roadside, he could still sense that the flowers were waving at him, cheering him on, encouraging him to show strength, willpower and his dance on the bike.

As a brick wall in front him, the fans stood wild and crazy only to disappear in that very moment they almost collided. In a surrealistic frenzy of sweat and insanity he forced his pedals around and he sensed how shoes, pedals and legs were all one and created one magnificent force.

He remembered his time as a child, how he had been standing there cheering when his own idols had passed by. He focused his mind on his biggest hero, who right in front of him had changed his gears, and had accelerated with a commanding stride away from his competitors. Today he was back and today it would be his turn to do this.

He checked in on his body one more time to make sure that it was ready. He filled his lungs with air and then he exploded with a gale force, almost not human here so close to top, so long into the stage, so hot in temperature, so totally crazy in this inferno of roaring fans.

He could feel it in his body and hear it in his ears that the reaction from the crowd was exactly as expected. Their exulted screams mounted to new heights and their cheers almost pushed his back. He could see the lens of the TV-camera on the motorcycle in front of him and he could see that it was focusing on his eyes and he himself focused on the little dark spot in the middle of the lens, just as he had imagined on the many training rides in all weather conditions he had made up this mountain. This was his mountain, he owned it!

He was so close to finishing his work and he felt the lactic acid in his legs. Funny enough the acid was neutralized by the cheering crowd and his own sensation of speed. He could feel that there was no one behind him anymore and that feeling made him push the pedals even harder. He shifted his gear again and got up and out of the saddle and allowed yet one more explosion, which in turn was rewarded by the ecstatic crowd, who now sensed that they were witnessing something spectacular, something historic, something of colossal importance, something that would be remembered and they were there to witness it.

He looked up, his face torn, but between brine, sweat, dust and deep furrows, there was also a smile. This is life he thought, nothing could be better and although working on the edge of exhaustion, he wished the mountain would never end, that he could just keep riding up and up and up, into the sky and that the crowd, now held back by iron fences on the last two kilometers, would come closer, enclose him and his performance.

He sensed that his body had even more to give and he felt convinced that regardless of who might be behind him, they were far away. He felt stronger and more invincible than ever before.

He knew that after the last turn there would be the steepest climb of the day, climbing at around 20 percent. He laughed out loud and tensed his muscular body as he turned into the last turn and invested all of his remaining energy in yet another explosion that left the crowd stunned and although cheering they were almost silent with awe, jaws dropped down. Or was it just his imagination? Was it that he didn't hear anything anymore? Time stood still and sounds disappeared.

Everything around him passed in slow motion. He heard an obscure sound in his ear, almost like a voice being played back too slow.

He could see the finish line and he pushed his pedals with all he had for this insane last climb. But it was as if he didn't move and that the finish line only came closer ever so slowly, now so near and yet so far away. A voice inside him yelled "NOW" and he raised his arms towards the sky and his eardrums almost burst under the sound wave that suddenly came rolling over him. He was caught by a soignior and he fell over his bike. He sensed there was no air in his lungs and he started hyperventilating. His legs were shaking and tears were coming from the corners of his eyes. His whole body was trembling and his legs, that a few seconds before had represented a veritable powerhouse, gave in under him.

Photographers and journalists pushed their cameras and microphones in his face and questions were hitting him like a hailstorm. He tried to answer, but was for once short of words. In the corner of his eyes he saw a familiar figure, his beloved wife and life support with their boy on her arm. He embraced her, sobbing and at this moment he let go of all his feelings.

A dirty face approached him. It was his good buddy and training partner who with a big smirk on his face congratulated him. He had been with him all the way, sitting right behind him on his rear wheel protecting him until the final decisive move when he no longer had the power to follow. He felt the recognizing pat on his shoulder and he knew that he could get no bigger reward. He was now the king of the mountain. He had just made his ultimate life goal come true and he felt happiness intoxicating his whole body.

He had his face washed by the soignoir and he followed race officials to the mandatory doping control. This was just something that had to be done and then he would again face the crowd and be on the top of the podium. While he was waiting behind the podium, his thoughts suddenly went to tomorrow. Tomorrow's stage had less altitude meters but yet invited new endeavors. He started focusing on the endless climbs that had to be passed and instinctively he sensed his legs. Were they alright? And then he sipped an extra sip of his coke as a compliment to his muscle mass. He felt ready, here only a few minutes after the ultimate unleashing of his inner self. He was at the top and he knew he was on his way to create something big.

He thought of showering and he thought of a bed, where he could be alone and concentrate on the new challenges tomorrow would bring. He thought of that wonderful happy feeling he would have when he was passing every little bump of tomorrow's stage. He was ready and he wanted to be challenged. It would be fun if some of the others could follow his first explosion, he thought to himself as he went on to the podium to receive the crowd's tribute.

3 HAPPINESS AND ALL THAT JAZZ

More than anything else man seeks happiness! *Hippocrates, year 300 B.C.*

Well, if happiness is so important and man forever has been searching for it, then maybe we should examine what happiness is and also what it is not. Let's start looking at what happiness is not…

Happiness is not something that just happens, meaning you have to have a mind-set that can support happiness; otherwise it will not be there.

Happiness does not happen because of luck or coincidences. In other words, you have to make an effort in order to be truly happy.

Happiness cannot be bought for money or ordered by authorities, which is one of the really interesting aspects of happiness, because so many people try to buy stuff in order to experience that good feeling. In reality happiness does not relate to money or income. In fact, many "poor" people may experience a more real sense of happiness because their happiness is less dependent on certain bought actions or costly behaviors.

Happiness is not a result of external causes but is dependent upon how we interpret external events. Happiness is a product of your own inner self and the way you choose to interpret the world around you. People can look at the same event and their mental filters will determine what they see and hear, so that the exact same experience has several different meanings.

Happiness is a state that must be prepared, cultivated and defended by each individual human being, and as such will not truly happen to a complacent person.

Happiness comes from being able to control internal experiences and through that determine the quality of your life. So the better you can control your mind and the way you choose to use it, the bigger the chance of finding real happiness.

Happiness is found by fully engaging us in every little part of our lives and it doesn't come as a side effect of pursuing a cause bigger than yourself! This perhaps is worth noting. Many people engage in activities where they will do a lot of good for others. In spite what most people will admit to, the real reason for doing this is not what the activity does for the others that is the real motivator, but rather the feeling of internal satisfaction that it gives the person doing the activity of helping others. All human behavior is driven by a positive intention and there is always a question to be asked consciously or unconsciously, "What's in it for me?", that will determine if the person engages in the activity or not.

When you engage in an activity there are moments that are better than others and there are the moments where you experience the Optimal Experience. These are the moments where you, instead of letting yourself be controlled by blind forces, feel in control of your own actions and destiny. It is those rare occasions where you are caught by a feeling of excitement, a feeling of happiness that you can treasure for a long time. These occasions will stay in your memory as expressions of how life ought to be.

The best moments in our life are not passive, receptive or relaxed. We have worked hard for them. They typically come when our body or mind is stretched to the limit in an attempt to achieve something difficult and valuable. So, we can say that Optimal Experiences are something we make happen!

Optimal Experience is the result of development and every single person has thousands of possibilities and challenges that can serve as development! We can also add that Optimal Experiences equal Flow – a state where people are so engaged in an activity that all others don't seem to matter. The experience in itself is so enjoyable that people would do the work because they enjoy it, even if it would cost them money.

When information interrupts consciousness by threatening its goals, there is a state of disorder or Mental Entropy, a disturbance of the self, limiting its efficiency. Long-lasting experiences of this kind can weaken the self in such a way that it no longer is capable of performing attention and pursuing its goals. So we can conclude that Mental Entropy is the opposite of Flow, the Optimal Experience.

When the information that streams into consciousness serves your goals, the mental energy can flow effortlessly. There is no need to worry, no need to question one's self worth. When one stops and thinks about one's self, it will cheerfully sound or feel "You are doing great". The positive feedback strengthens the self and more attention is released to take care of the outer and inner environment.

After each flow episode a person will grow to an even more unique individual with new and, until now, unknown skills. When the flow event is over, you feel more whole than before, not just internally but also in relation to other people and the world in general. The self becomes more complex by experiencing flow and the complexity contributes to new growth.

In our pursuit of happiness we can also have experiences of Joy and Pleasure. Joy is a feeling of satisfaction that you experience when the information in your conscious mind tells you that the expectations that your biological programs and your social conditioning has set, have been met. Pleasure occurs when a person has not only delivered upon expectations or satisfied a need or a lust, but furthermore has moved past what it is programmed to do and has reached something unexpected, previously not even perceived possible.

As it may already have become clear to you, Flow is not about what you do but rather how you do it. People have had Flow in the weirdest of contexts but because of their ability to devote and engage in a given activity, they have managed to push all other matters aside in their mind and focus on what they were doing and not the surrounding circumstances on which they may not have had any influence on at all. Or in some cases, they may even have been deprived of any control of their external environment yet have had the mental power to achieve Flow.

One very important aspect in achieving Flow is knowing the direction in which you are going, in other words, having a goal. Autotel comes from the two Greek words auto that means self, and telos that means goal. Autotel is an activity that rests in its self, an activity that is performed without any expectations about later rewards, but simply done because the act of doing it, in itself, carries the reward. When an experience is Autotel, the person will direct their attention towards the activity for the sake of the activity alone.

This of course also means that if you do an activity only to please others, it will be very hard if not impossible to experience Flow in that activity. Another question is, if you only do the activity to please others and you keep doing it without enjoying it and with nothing in it for yourself other than pleasing others, then how will that influence your self-esteem over time?

To quote Dr. Richard Bandler, self-esteem comes from feeling good, which comes from doing the right things for the right reasons. If the act of doing it, in itself, does not carry the reward for you it will not be the right reason and the right thing and thus not generate the good feeling. Without the good feeling, no Flow.

4 PERCEPTION

People are surrounded by information which is received by our brain and reprogrammed into something understandable and then processed into actions in the form of internal as well as external reactions.

Just how the human brain performs this process and the influence it has had on our doing and actions have been the subject of discussion and research for thousands of years. Even as far back as Plato, and perhaps even further back people have philosophized about this subject.

In the modern age, a psychologist named Alfred Korzybski founded a school (General Semantics) around the way we look at this process. Based on his work, the first half of the 1970's saw the creation of a revised and expanded model that we will use as a starting point.

Korzybski wrote "We do not see the world as it really is, but a generalized model of it." This means that what we think we see does not necessarily reflect the actual facts.

The reason for this is to be found in the process performed by the human mind when provided with information. Information means all the impressions we come across and that our five senses can perceive.

German scientist Alfred Zimmerman (1993) has measured that approximately 310 million units of information per second is being poured in over us and is being picked up by our various sensory channels. Of these 310 million units of information, our unconscious part of the brain can process around 11.2 million units of information per second (Zimmerman 1993, Nørretranders 1994) and our conscious mind can only handle approximately 40 units of information per second. In the 1950's George Miller concluded that our consciousness can only operate with seven plus or minus two units of information at the same time. So how does the brain figure out how to process this and what do with the information?

To complete this task, the human brain has a "filter", the purpose of which is to reduce or funnel the many millions of bits down to the 40 bits that the conscious part of the brain can handle. You can consider this scenario somewhat like your computer. There is the hard drive which stores all the information and then there is the RAM which is the operational part of the computer. The designers of the computer have actually modeled the human mind, perhaps even without knowing this consciously!

The information is filtered in three steps as follows:

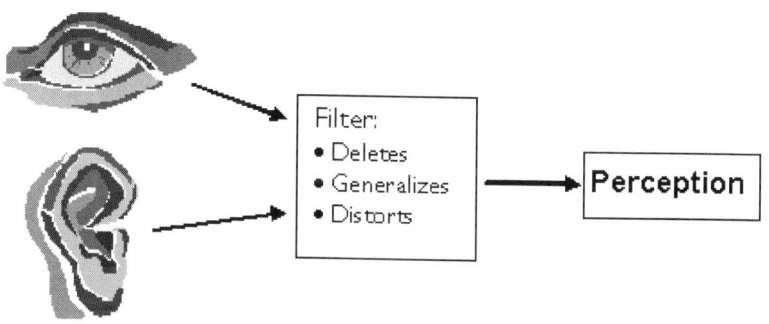

In the first part of the funneling process all the information deemed not to be significant is excluded from our consciousness. An example of this is when you find yourself in a room full of other people. If you listen to every word, everyone in the room says, it would most likely be an inferno of voices and sounds. If, however, you start a conversation with another person, you will focus on his or her voice and hear that while sending all the other audible information to the back of your consciousness.

In the second part of the funneling process is the activity of generalizing. We will organize a range of information and contract that into one piece of information to create clarity. Let us use a house as an example. When you look at a house, your brain receives loads of information in respect to building materials and structures, windows, etc. But instead of mentioning all these parts, we simply say "a house". We may choose to focus on an individual part of the house and bring more details to the fore of our consciousness, or we may choose to look at a concentration of houses as a city instead of a lot of individual houses. This allows us to describe things more quickly to ourselves and others.

The information you receive is interpreted in the way that you have been taught to interpret it, through influences from your surroundings. The Cuban missile crisis serves as an example. The printed media (newspapers) in the USA or Soviet Union probably described the course of events differently. Based on the information you as a reader receive, you will influence your perception of right and wrong under the circumstances. Politics and religion are very strong influencing factors, just to mention a few, but every day you are influenced by sources sending information to you and this has been happening since you were born. In fact families may be some of the biggest influencers of all.

After the information needed has been chosen, grouped into categories that we can relate to and then interpreted, we end up with the end result which then again will cause us to react. When we react, our reactions will again pass through the filter, so that the output is also controlled by what we perceive necessary for the recipient. It will be based on how we categorize and it will be based on our values and beliefs.

No two filters operate in the same way! As no two people focus on the exact same thing with the exact same senses, nor possess the exact same contraction of information or receive the exact same influence throughout their lives. No two people filter or think alike. Some people may have very identical thoughts and generally be on similar "wavelengths", but they will never think in the exact same way in every respect!

This means that all human beings are mentally unique and hence that everyone has an individual perception of what goes on in a specific situation. Let us use the police officer interrogating witnesses to a traffic accident for his report as an example. The witnesses' statements will be influenced by what they focused on, what they have been taught about traffic behavior and their general perception of right and wrong.

In a workplace or in a relationship, this means that you cannot assume that everybody else knows what you are thinking and saying, as their perception depends on the way their filters process the information that you send out.

By appreciating this process and what it does to your perception of the world around you, you may find it easier to understand why other people sometimes disagree with you – even on topics that to you are obvious – to other are they not – or what?

The fact is that a fact can be defined as a thing that the people discussing it can agree to. In other words, if two people agree on a certain thing this may then represent a fact for them, but not to the onlooker or third party. Political or religious conflicts are a sure sign of this. What is the most obvious and true in one religion or to one particular political conviction may be considered a lie or not true for the other.

5 FLOW AND THE STRUCTURE OF THINKING

In reality all people can experience Flow, so why look at the structures of thinking? Well simply because some ways of thinking can promote Flow and if you practice thinking in that way, you can set yourself in the right direction.

Let's first define what Thinking Structures are. In terms of changeability of the human mind, we can establish the following sequence, starting from what is easiest to influence and change and ending up with the most difficult if at all possible to influence or change.

The fastest thing to change in a human mind is Attention. If you are looking in a particular direction and a sudden loud sound comes from another direction you shift your attention immediately. Should there be a new sudden loud sound in a different direction, then you probably shift your attention again. Easy to influence but also hard to maintain.

The second layer is your Knowledge. You can read something and obtain the knowledge. Knowledge does not mean that you are capable of doing it, but only refers to that you do know the principles of how it works. Although there can be a difference in what kind of knowledge different people can absorb the best, generally speaking it is still easy to change the level of knowledge. Obviously you need to put your attention first to the topic, so already here we can establish some kind of sequence.

The third level is Skills. Requiring skills, means that you have to be able to do it. This requires not only attention and knowledge but now also practice. Knowing is not doing and this is seen so many times in management where different training concepts have been offered to managers, but with too little practice never materialize as skills and as such are not recognized in behavior although the knowledge is there.

The fourth level is where we come across Thinking Structures. These are what I call the daily behavior drivers. They are contextual and are driven by the contextual values and beliefs. They can be deeply rooted due to long exposure to a certain set of values and beliefs, but as with any value and belief, they can be influenced and thus changed. The thing that separates humans from other species is no doubt our ability to adapt ourselves to shifting environments and this is also what happens to our behavior. We enter a new environment and when we do so we come in with a certain set of values and beliefs, based upon what we previously have been exposed to. And then, if we stay long enough, we will gradually adapt the new set of contextual values and beliefs. It may differ a lot from person to person, how long a time it takes will depend upon how far the new set of values and beliefs are from what set we held before entering the new environment.

The fifth and sixth level are by some considered one and by others two separate levels. For the sake of listing them I have chosen to separate them but in reality it is not so important.

The fifth level is the one of personal dynamics. This is your emotional response pattern and can be traced back thousands of years ago when the first diagnostic approach was related to your emotional response to things happening around you.

Finally the sixth level is the one of personality and this is being argued whether this is genetic heritage or environmental and for the sake of this book I will not devote time to that discussion, but rather conclude that most – but absolutely not all – scientists and researchers seem to agree that the fifth and the sixth level are not at all or at least are very hard to influence or change. As Thinking Structures can be influenced and changed I have chosen to work with them, as this seems to be more relevant.

It is very important to remember that Thinking Structure preferences are not personality and thus they can and may be changed and even more important to remember – they are contextual. That means that preferences in one context may not be the same preferences in any other context, and things happening inside any given context can influence a person to change some or several of the preferences.

Each category or thinking structure has a number of preferences. For example the thinking structure "Direction" has the two preferences "Towards" and "Away-from".

Depending on your approach to Thinking Structures or Meta Programs as they are originally called, you will find them listed in many different ways. In terms of Flow, I have chosen to use the definitions from the LAB Profile by Rodger Bailey (Language and Behavior Profile, see "Words That Change Minds" by Canadian author Shelle Rose Charvet for a deeper insight), as this is an easy to comprehend and use method. The LAB Profile is divided into two sections of which the first is all about motivation and therefore particularly useful when talking about Flow.

In the following we will discuss the various categories (thinking structures) and the belonging preferences and their influence on flow.

Motivation Traits

The first part of the LAB Profile deals with motivation and as such the most important when talking about Flow. There are 6 different categories or thinking structures in motivation and I will present them in the order they appear in the profile and not in any given priority towards Flow.

Level

Does a person take the initiative or wait for others? There are two preferences inside the category. You can be **Proactive** and be motivated by doing and acting with little or no consideration or you can be **Reactive** and motivated by waiting, analyzing, considering and then reacting.

You can argue if any of these have a specific influence on the ability to generate Flow, but there is no doubt that the one who seeks will experience Flow more often and as such being too reactive means that you wait for others to take initiative. This may in turn mean that you do not get your things done but only think about doing them and as such do not get around to pursuing your goals.

Criteria

These words are a person's labels for goodness, rightness and appropriateness in a given context. They incite a positive physical and emotional reaction. They are labels for values.

Criteria, or values as I prefer to call them, are very important when talking about Flow. By knowing what your values are and living them fully you are much closer to experience Flow, than if you are struggling with an imbalance or confusion in what is important to you and what you do. If these do not match, you will have an inner conflict which may mean mental entropy and therefore be the opposite of Flow.

Direction

Is a person's motivational energy centered on goals or problems? This could also be defined as the search for achieving or avoiding. People who are **Towards** are motivated more by achieving or attaining goals and people who are **Away From** are more motivated to solve problems and focus on what's wrong.

Having clear goals is a must for finding the state of Flow and, generally speaking, goals that are well formed and targeted towards achievement have a bigger chance of being reached. Being towards will therefore be to your advantage en route to Flow (hereby not saying that people with an Away From preference cannot get into Flow). Another prerequisite for Flow is your ability to stay focused, to concentrate. This means that you have to be able to prioritize and not let yourself get detoured and off track. People who are away from may have trouble staying focused on goals and may find themselves being detoured by attention to a problem. People who are towards are very good at staying focused but may have trouble recognizing problems, so the optimal combination could be towards with some away from, so that you do stay focused but is not blind to what could go wrong.

Source

Does a person become motivated by judgments from external sources or by using their own internal standards? Being **Internal** means that you decide based on your own internal standards and being **External** means that you need outside feedback to make judgments. Being able to monitor how well you are doing yourself allows for faster learning as you do not have to wait for other people's feedback. And, it also allows you to realize when you are achieving your goals faster. This means that it could be to your advantage to be more internal. Obviously the ideal combination is towards and internal in terms of being committed to reaching your target. If we look at high performers there is little doubt that many of these have this combination. Given too much of each of these two preferences could lead people to act egocentrically which does not necessarily prevent Flow. On the contrary, it could lead to being so focused that you may suddenly find yourself pursuing in the wrong direction but not listening to the external feedback telling you this.

Reason

Does a person continually look for alternatives or prefer to follow established procedures? People with a preference for **Options** are compelled to develop and create other procedures and systems. The may have difficulty following set procedures and they may also have difficulty in making decisions as any decision may limit their options. People with a preference for **Procedures** prefer to follow and complete a set procedure. They can get stuck when they have no procedure to follow.

Being able to follow a procedure also means that what is begun should be finished. This ability can be very important in a determined pursuit of goals. Not being good at following procedures may mean that new options appearing potentially can sidetrack you and thus take you away from your plan and target. In sports it is crucial to success to follow some kind of training regime and with options as a preference this will typically be changed all the time and not allow the necessary repetitions in any given system. However, it is important to say that with too much procedure as a preference you may get stuck in a dysfunctional routine and not be able to shift to a new and more functional one.

Decision Factors

How does a person react to change and what frequency of change do they need? Not everyone likes change. In fact, many people are to some degree afraid of change. This is possibly rooted in the basic fear of the unknown, by some said to be the biggest fear of mankind. However, because the unknown is so feared it may also help motivate one to change if that change can help maintain the known. So talking about change is a complex matter.

We do know that there is a big difference though on how often people feel the need for change and we can divide this need into four different preferences. **Sameness** people want their world to stay the same. They will provoke change every 15 to 25 years. They are very comfortable with the familiar and are good at maintaining the familiar. People with a preference for **Sameness with Exception** prefer situations to evolve slowly over time. They want major change every 5 to 7 years. These people prefer an evolutionary approach to change and accept time as a factor for change. People with a **Difference** preference want change to be constant and drastic. They need a major change every 1 to 2 years and sometimes even faster. **Sameness with Exception and Difference** people like evolution and revolution. Major change will happen on average every 3 years.

Since Skills and Flow are very closely related, evolution can be seen as contributing factor to Flow. However, as Mihaly Csikszentmihalyi points out with several examples in his books on Flow, many people find Flow in cultivating a certain thing for years and years, so maintaining can also be seen as supportive. If the need is for difference or sameness with exception and difference there can be a rush for learning and conquering new skills and the pursuit of this can lead to Flow.

We can say that the category is closely linked to comfort and whatever produces the most comfort for you is good as long as it can support your goals. If it hinders your goals it can lead to mental entropy and as such prevent Flow.

In terms of motivation traits, we can sum up and say that looking for the ideal combination of preferences it could appear that having clear criteria that can guide you in the pursuit towards your goals and not waiting for others to initiate can be supporting for experiencing Flow. Having a system for evaluation is crucial and this has to be controlled from the inside, but containing some kind of external input as well as having an external control mechanism could be beneficial. Finishing what's started is crucial and this requires a procedural approach and the combining of this with an approach to change that is evolutionary will support the gradual skill building often needed to experience Flow at very high levels.

It is perhaps worth noting that Flow can be experienced at all skill levels and for many learning a new thing can certainly lead to some kind of Flow experience, although not as profound as the ones experienced at a higher levels where more effort has been put into the experience.

We know from the world of sports that a phenomenon like Runners High comes from chemicals accumulated in the brain. The continued effort produces Endorphins which has a huge impact on your mood. As Flow equals the optimal experience and happiness is connected to this, the pursuit of happiness can be helped by physical training. So even if your pursuit of Flow is in something not related to sports you can assist your brain by serious physical training. And this combined with your ability to motivate yourself and understand what is required for you to stay motivated can be a determining factor for Flow.

Working Traits

The second half of the LAB Profile is linked to how you process information and although very interesting it is not as relevant for Flow as the first part. There are however a couple of the categories that I find worthwhile mentioning as this will influence how you process the information that you need in order to build skills.

Scope

How large a picture is the person able to work with? A person who is **Specific** needs details and sequences. They may not see the overview. This may lead to a fantastic ability to focus on a particular detail but forgetting the overall plan and not prioritizing time accordingly. A person who is **General** needs overview, the big picture. This person can handle details for short periods of time.

If a person is too general they may not devote enough time to develop their skills to perfection. So, it appears that some attention to detail is needed. According to the LAB Profile norm groups (North American), most people are general in their preference. So the question is how long they can attend to details. Practicing focusing on details for a longer period of time may be recommended.

Stress Response

How does a person react to the normal stresses of the work environment? This has a lot to do with your ability to associate into and dissociate from your feelings. You can argue what is the most useful but there is little doubt that getting into Flow requires determination and as such some attached emotions to the activity you are doing. We have seen it over and over again in athletes. Some are very emotional even to the extent where they cannot control this and then we have witnessed people who appeared to be cool as cucumbers only to lose control when triggered the right way. There can be little doubt that if you are too controlled by emotions this could be a potential risk on the other hand a lot of the energy comes from being absorbed and attached.

People with a preference for **Feelings** have emotional responses to normal levels of stress. They stay in feelings and may not be suited for long term high-stress work as this will tear them apart from the inside. People with a **Choice** preference can move in and out of feelings voluntarily. They are good at empathy, and this may be to their advantage as long as empathy does not control them so that they withhold themselves in the activity they wish to do. The third preference is the **Thinking preference**. These are people who do not go into feelings at normal levels of stress. This is a somewhat emotionally detached preference and these people are very good at staying cool even under very stressed circumstances. The only question here is if they can be committed enough with this detachment from emotions.

Style

What kind of human environment allows a person to work best? This can be a very important category because if ignored could lead to the wrong environment for the activity which again will lead to mental entropy.

People with an **Independent** preference prefer to work alone with sole responsibility. They may not be very productive if they have to work in groups although they can.

People with a preference for **Proximity** prefer to be in control of own territory with others around them. This means that if they are on their own for too long this may influence motivation. People with a **Co-operative** preference enjoys working together with others in a team, sharing responsibility and they do not function well if left alone or have to make independent decisions. All of these can have the experience as long as they have the optimal environment for their activities.

Rule Structure

Does a person have rules for themselves and others? This one is particularly interesting from the skills perspective, because it also deals with whether you know how to get better or not. Not knowing may not be a problem if you have are motivated by an external source, however if you have to wait all the time for other people to tell you what to do, chances are slim that you will experience Flow. Knowing how to get better and pursuing that, is one of the core aspects of getting into Flow, not just once, but over and over again as you build your skills and challenge yourself more and more.

People with a **My/My** preference will say My rules for me. My rules for you. They are also able to tell others what they expect and as such can make good leaders. People with a **My/.** preference will say My rules for me. I don't care about you. People with a **My/Your** preference will say My rules for me. Your rules for you. They are hesitant to tell others what to do, but this is no problem in terms of Flow as long as the activity in which they engage themselves in is not related to telling others what to do (managers etc.) All three of these preferences share the fact that they do know how to get better and depending on the type of activity they engage in it may not be relevant if they can tell others or not.

People with a **No/My** preference will say Don't know rules for me. My rules for you. This means they have no rules for themselves and as such do not know how to improve their skills. Because they have rules for others, it may be a challenge to convince them about how to improve unless they have a strong external source preference and as such will gladly accept expert advice.

Convincer Mode

What has to happen to the information or evidence previously gathered so that a person becomes "convinced" of something? This is interesting from the perspective of happiness. Can you experience real happiness if you are never convinced about your own abilities?

There are four preferences and the two of them seems to fall in the same category and they are **Number of Examples** where they need to have the data a certain number of times to be convinced and **Period of Time** where they need to gather information for a certain duration before their conviction is triggered. Both of these should have no challenges in experiencing Flow.

People with an **Automatic** preference will take a small amount of information and get convinced immediately based on what they extrapolate. They hardly ever change their minds. These people may have a challenge if they too quickly decide they know it all about their chosen activity or needs to shift approach in order to move on to the next level.

People who have a **Consistent** preference are facing a very different challenge that may or may not work to their advantage. These people are never completely convinced. Every day is a new day and they need to get re-convinced. Now this can work to the advantage where this preference is not too strong or dominant because it will lead them to a constant pursuit of skill building and challenge and in the right amount can be stimulating for the Flow scenario. However given too strong a preference they may experience a feeling of dissatisfaction because they are never good enough, never convinced about their own abilities and this means that even though all the other prerequisites are present in terms of experiencing Flow, their experience will not be that great and they will not enjoy the moment enough to call it Flow!

There are many other Meta Programs or Thinking Structures if you like and the above have been chosen for their relevance to the Flow experience.

When working with Meta Programs/Thinking Structures it cannot be stressed enough that these do not operate in the same way as the concept of personality. Most researchers seem to agree that personality does not change after the age of around 20-22 years of age. Well, whether that is true or not I will leave to others to discuss, but we do know that behavior is contextual and although some behavior seems to be generated or caused by deeply rooted things stemming from personality, we can also see that the ability of the human race to adapt means that contextual values and beliefs have a stronger influence on behavior in most cases and therefore are more relevant to look at when dealing with Flow and behavior in general.

6 THE FORMULA FOR FLOW

One of the things that inspired me to write this book was the fact that in all his books on Flow Mihaly Csikszentmihalyi talked about Flow as something you could not truly influence and generate yourself, but that Flow was rather a state that occurred from time to time as a result of things done. Reading through his books however there is a pattern of the prerequisites for Flow and these are:

1. Create a compelling goal and make the appropriate number of realistic sub-goals (Milestones)

2. Find ways to measure progress according to the chosen goals

3. Concentration about what you are doing and constantly raise the challenges that the activity gives you

4. Develop the necessary skills that make you able to do the activity

5. Keep raising the stakes if the activity starts to bore you.

So the question is to me, what are the active parts that we can do in order to promote the chance of getting into Flow?

Well the way you think about things and the way you perceive the world around you are for sure determining factors as we have just discussed in the previous two chapters. But, the overall theme for Flow is to balance your skills and the challenges you have and gradually raise the bar so that you, at all times, have the optimal situation where you are challenged accordingly to your skill level to the extent where your skills are stretched but sufficient. And then, at all times, keep that balance, which in reality means raising the challenge bar and the skills bar one at a time, but not always in that specific order.

Modified "Flow" Model
Created by H. Arne Maus, based on Mihalyi Csikszentmihalyi & Norbert Bischof

In A1 there is a balance between challenges and skills and although challenges are low so are the skills and as such a match. So, it is possible to experience Flow even when you are starting out on a new activity.

In A2 you have now acquired skills to the extent where there is no more any challenge in the activity and doing the activity has begun to bore you. If you continue in this direction you can experience a kind of stress that comes from being bored too much for too long and in the extreme it could lead to Bore out.

In A3 you have too many challenges and too few resources and/or skills and this leads to stress and in some cases to Burnout.
Both A2 and A3 are highly demotivating states to be in but even worse is that it can lead to mental states where a person becomes dysfunctional and may need expert help and counseling or in some cases hospitalization.

In A4 there is again a balance between challenges and skills but this time at a much higher level and as you can see the zone opens up a little into a wedge, meaning that the chance of experiencing Flow increases the more you dedicate yourself to mastery.

One could only start to imagine how the world would look like of more managers started leading their people with Flow in mind! Imagine being challenged to a point where the challenges meet your skill level and from time to time being stretched a little further but no further than what you had a chance to have your skills build as well to go along with the increase in challenges – what would that feel like? What would you think about the manager who was able to do just that?

Now I realize that some of you reading this book are not into management but rather aim at managing yourself and your own growth and here the importance is that you are able to recognize the symptoms of being inside or outside the wedge. If you are outside, then develop the knowledge and wisdom on what can get you back into the wedge.

As you can see from the formula another important criteria is concentration. Concentration is to a large degree generated through the challenges which any activity will give us. In other words, it is the challenges that give us the level of concentration that may be needed. If something seems to be too easy, it often leads to less concentration, Whereas, things perceived difficult will generate high concentration. Errors and mistakes are therefore often due to lack of challenges or concentration and if there is little concentration this most often indicates lack of motivation! If an activity feels like something you "Have to do" it is also difficult - if not impossible - to reach a state of flow.

In essence it all comes down to having enough mental strength and control to make activities to something you would like to do; no matter if it at the same time is something you have to do. If challenges are missing, this can be difficult, so you have to create goals that will give you challenges, so that it can be a good and positive experience to reach the goal and so that reaching the goal, will feel like giving your life quality.

7 USING MENTAL TRAINING TO PROMOTE FLOW

When reading about Flow one of the things I noticed is how fixed many people in the world of psychology seem to be on limitations of the human mind, when in fact one of the most limitless things there is, is in fact the human mind.

Think about it for a moment. If the human mind were not indeed limitless, how did we ever end up going to the moon? How come it was possible to conceive of such a plan if not somebody somewhere said "That's possible"?

To me it is as if the field of psychology deals with the human mind as some sort of a limiting beliefs machine and observing it from a limiting belief. Now I know that this is a huge generalization and many people inside psychology have started changing that approach, but yet we still find that most of the literature is about what the human mind is not capable of. when, in fact, the very resources to development and progress lies more between the ears then between the hands of the person what he or she is doing. By saying that we are not capable of we are holding on to a belief almost identical to the one of the planet earth not being round. Luckily somebody challenged that belief and low and behold – they were right.

The human mind and body are probably the most complex things there are on this planet. The cell structure in the human body alone is an astonishing thing, with approximately 50 trillion cells according to Bruce Lipton Ph.D. recreating themselves over and over again and each one of them with a conscious and an unconscious mind.

The brain's and the nervous system's capacity to find new ways around damaged areas in the brain and in ruptured nerves is amazing, bringing back functionality in areas otherwise damaged for good and then we talk about limits of the human mind!

Think of the world of sports. Performance enhancing drugs are now being used in most sports and people are willing to experiment with their vital organs in the pursuit of victory and gold. But at the same time they are not spending time or devoting themselves to how much more they could achieve with systematic mental training. In fact many coaches in today's world of sports are very similar to the people some 500 years hundred years ago who demanded people jailed, flogged or burned on the bonfire for saying that the earth was round. They hold beliefs that mental training is a waste of time and or some kind of voodoo only performed in primitive societies.

One of the few fields that has dared to go against this stream is the field of Neuro-Linguistic Programming. The inventors of the field dared going against the established beliefs in the field of psychology and for this reason they too were treated like the people who claimed that the Earth was round and not flat. Many of their initial claims are now household knowledge and one can only wonder why some people still spend so much energy on arguing against a field that has proven to help so many people around the world.

Neuro-Linguistic Programming™ or NLP as I will refer to it from now on is the study and modeling of human behavior. *"**NLP is an Attitude** characterized by the sense of curiosity and adventure and a desire to learn the skills to be able to find out what kinds of communication influences somebody and the kind of things worth knowing... to look at life as a rare and unprecedented opportunity to learn.* **NLP is a Methodology** *based on the overall operational presupposition that all behavior has a structure... and that structure can be modeled, learned, taught, and changed (reprogrammed). The way to know what will be useful and effective are the perceptual skills.* **NLP has evolved as an innovative Technology** *enabling the practitioner to organize information and perceptions in ways that allow them to achieve results that were once inconceivable."* Quote from Richard Bandler, Co-Creator of NLP.

NLP is based on the three core components. Neuro refers to the nervous system through which experience is received and processed through the five senses. Linguistic refers to language and nonverbal communication systems through which neural representations are coded, ordered, and then given meaning. And Programming refers to the ability to organize our communication and neurological systems to achieve specific desired goals and results.

NLP has existed since the early seventies and many people have contributed to the development of the field. The techniques in this book come from many of these and it is the sequencing of these techniques that I can contribute. As much as possible I will refer to the originator of each exercise in order to give due credit to the right person. However, there is one person who deserves a special credit for his ability to be curious enough to do what others dared not and that is Dr. Richard Bandler who is the co-creator of NLP. More than any other he has contributed to what the field is today. Many others have claimed their fame and their right to his ideas and his discoveries but no one has so consistently contributed to new insights to human behavior and the way we can influence this as Richard has. It would not be fair to write a book using the Methodology and Technology of NLP without mentioning and honoring his contributions.

To some, the Earth is still flat in terms of human behavior, but to others, they have found not only that the Earth is round but also that it belongs to a solar system that does not evolve around Earth but rather where the Earth is but a part. As such, I invite you to become part of that smarter population who allows results and opportunity to open up your door to the possible, to the world where limiting beliefs are for others who dare not, and where your success is linked to your personal drive for happiness and optimal experiences, not held back by conventional beliefs but propelled forward by your own desire to achieve.

In the following chapters I will introduce to you techniques that step by step can help you towards the Flow experience. They cannot guarantee your success because so many factors may influence it, but they certainly can enhance your chances of success.

As with any other skill, mental training and the application of NLP requires practice and without it you may not succeed as wildly as possible. This means that the techniques introduced and the exercises given must be done, most of them more than once, in order to gain competency. And for some of them, it may be to your advantage to have somebody else guide you through them so that you can concentrate on the experience itself. Whenever this is advisable this will be clearly highlighted in order for you to maximize your outcome from this book. Obviously, if you have access to an experienced NLP Practitioner, they would be the optimal training partner. However, all exercises can be done by yourself.

Mental training requires as much effort as any other skill. And for the serious athlete, or whatever your activity is, you should devote time to regular practice of your mental skills. This is very often overlooked or not considered necessary, but it is.

To use a quote from the book "Using Your Brain For A Change" by Dr. Richard Bandler, he says "Most people spend more time learning to use their remote control than they spend learning how to operate their brain" and this is very much the sad truth. Much of what I have written here ought to be included in biology classes in Grammar School, but is not even taught at college level. I introduced the perception process and the structure of thinking to some colleagues recently and one of them responded, "Why are we not taught this in school?" and I could only agree with her – it is a mystery.

8 I HAVE A DREAM

Martin Luther King said these famous words and they have engraved themselves into history and so they should, because he was able to imagine how life could be. This imagination you can have too. All it requires is a little bit of structure and this is where we will start the adventure towards Flow.

If you do not have compelling goals that can fulfill your dreams, you will not get into Flow. Flow only happens when you are in pursuit of your goal and in order to have a goal worth striving for, you need to be able to imagine how it would be like to be there, so that you know what you are striving for.

Being creative and having creative compelling dreams are not for everyone. Some people have a combination of Thinking Structures where they are good at getting ideas but then also equally good at criticizing them, so that the ideas are shot down before they even get a chance to fly.

Every creative project needs to incorporate the three aspects of creative imagination, practical action and critical refinement. One of the people who early on recognized this was Walt Disney who understood that these processes also have tough conditions if you try to do all three at the same time. How many times have you been part of a brain storming process where more time has been spent on criticizing the ideas, than on actually gathering ideas?

By making a distinct separation of the roles, it becomes easier to maximize the purpose of each of them. In a company you can have a specialist performing each of the three functions, so that everyone contributes to the role where they have the most to offer but as an individual, you need to have some capability in all three roles. Most of us are naturally stronger in one or two roles, and decidedly weaker in a third. The first step is having the self-awareness to recognize this. And the next is to commit to developing the skills necessary for that role.

Let's have a closer look at the three distinct roles. We will start off with The Dreamer. Ask yourself, "What am I trying to do or achieve?" and "If I could wave a magic wand and do anything I like – what would I create? How would it look? What could I do with it? How would that make me feel?"

Obviously when you ask yourself these questions you should be in place that invites bright ideas, not in a small dark and confined space. Go outside or face a window with a view or go for a walk in a nice inspiring environment, maybe out in the open or by the sea or whatever options you have. Just make sure that you feel relaxed and good, that you are in a mood where you can smile. This will generate the right kind of chemicals in your brain and body that can support your creativity.

Now in this space everything is possible and nothing is impossible. There are never bad ideas, just bad ways of carrying them out or not securing the quality, so allow yourself to go a little crazy, to imagine the best possible scenario. Do not attempt to make a plan for how to do it and do not look for what can go wrong, as we will look at these parts of the process later. So the trick is at this point to just allow yourself to dream about what you really, really want.

Once you have your dream and it feels compelling, then it is time to go to the next phase, which is called the Realist. Rightfully it could also be called the planner, because now it is time to create a plan that can make your dream come true. So find a place where you have what you need for planning. This may be flip charts or posters or calendars and markers. Whatever you need in order to plan efficiently and then ask yourself, "What steps do I need to go through to get there and what resources do I need to make this happen – people, money, materials and technology?" and "What is my timeline and where are the milestones?"

Now when the plan is laid out it is time once again to shift environment. Now it's time to become the Critic, which to me is also the Quality Controller. This time go to a dark, warm, sinister room (ha ha) and then, only looking at the plan for achieving the dream, ask yourself the following questions "Is this the best I/we can do? What would make it better?" and "Is there anything that could go wrong in this plan?" Check the timeline. Is it realistic, or are you dependent on luck or others, etc.?

Once you have noted what in the plan that needs to be different in order to make the plan better, then go back to the planning room or place and take a new look at the identified places where things can go wrong and then ask yourself "How can I then do this without having that problem?" Adjust the plan accordingly and also check if this requires any changes in the other things in your plan… could be you need to adjust your timeline, or skills you may need to pick up before you can go on to the next stage, etc.

Once you have that, step back to the place of the Critic/Quality Controller and run through the plan again and ask yourself "Is there anything that could go wrong in this revised plan?"

Circle through these two steps until there is nothing more that you see, hear, feel can go wrong in the plan.

Then go back to where you started and now look through the steps in your plan, revisit your dream and see if the plan is congruent with your dream or if it has moved too far away. Most often there will be an even better feeling associated with the dream, because now you know that it can be done!

When you feel satisfied, then go back to the place where you made the plan. Look in the direction of your future and mark out the milestones on the floor. So, where is the first step, the second step, the third step etc., all the way to your goal? Once you have that, step out onto the first milestone and see, hear, feel what it's like to be there, and if it is ok then step on to the next milestone, and so on until you reach your goals. This serves to double check your plan and if anything does not feel right, then take two or three steps to the side and become the neutral spectator, asking yourself from out there, looking into the step "What is not right? What needs to be changed?" Change it and step back and feel if it is better now and then proceed or adjust until right.

Beware of getting the roles mixed up! Stay focused on the purpose of each of the three roles. Moving from one distinct location for each role assists this. You can also place three pieces of paper on the floor and with some practice, you can do it sitting in the same chair, but I will recommend that you utilize space to help you – so move around, preferably from room to room, the first couple of times. If you intend to do this with more than one person, I will highly recommend that you move from room to room.

The exercise you just did is based on a technique developed by Robert Dilts who modeled Walt Disney and his approach to his creative genius. The technique utilized your ability to associate and dissociate in a way where association is used to make sure that this feels good and right and dissociation is used to gain perspective on the plan and see flaws that you may not see when totally engaged in the experience.

Now having completed the above exercise and having the finalized and quality controlled plan it is time to allow this dream to manifest, so find a comfortable place and position yourself in a comfortable way. It may be your favorite recliner or your bed or anything where you can feel good and relaxed.

First, take a deep breath in through your mouth and then hold it for a second and then slowly let it out through your nose and continue this way of breathing and notice how your pulse starts to slow down and you start to relax your muscles in the shoulders, arms, legs, feet, torso and head.

Now run the movie with your dream – the finalized version – all the way from where you started your journey and to the finish. Make the picture big and bright – like going to the IMAX theatre. Make it 3D, bring it in as close as comfort allows, and see yourself doing all the necessary steps towards your goal. See, hear and feel what it is like to see yourself completing these steps and for every good feeling that comes from seeing that, accept that this is your destiny and smile.

Exercise 1: Find a large piece of paper or a notebook and the write down the answers to the experiences you just had:

    1. **My dream is to:**

    2. **When I'm there what will it look like, sound like, feel like?**

    3. **My final plan to get there is:**

    4. **I have the following milestones in my plan (Set date wherever possible):**

Optional:

1. I found the following obstacles in my plan:

2. I made the following corrections to my plan:

The reason I am suggesting you write down identified obstacles and measures to counter them, is to remind you about these, so that you do not forget to get around them!

Exercise 2: Now make a movie of living your dream. Include living your plan and run it again and again and notice if there is anything that needs to be adjusted in order to feel even better.

9 WELL FORMED OUTCOMES

Once you have the dream and you know this is what you want to achieve, and have a fool-proof plan that will take you there, it is time to set goals for this dream. There are many methods to create a powerful goal. Here we will use "The Well Formed Outcomes" model. The Well Formed Outcomes model is a simple 5-step process. You should of course do this for the overall goal that is your dream, but also for each of the milestones (or we can call them sub goals). These are the ones that need to be accomplished in order to get you to the big goal.

Many people forget about the milestones and then try to get right to the end result in one go and that may be too ambitious and may not be very realistic. To illustrate this, think about a person trying to get to the top of Mount Everest. If you were standing at the foot of the mountain and strapped on your backpack and started walking, you probably wouldn't make it to the top. Actually chances are that you would die from exhaustion or altitude sickness. For this reason the route to the top has some camps along the way.

There is the base camp where people arrive and get organized and you can very much look at these exercises as your base camp. You are now in the process of getting ready to pursue your goals, fulfilling your dreams and experiencing Flow in the process of getting there. From there on it is on to the next camp. Stay there for a while, rest or regroup and then go onto the next, etc.

Now, sometimes you also have to stop and say, "Oops, it appears as if I am not on the right track." and then go back to the previous camp and get reorganized. Sometimes this means that you have to rest before you proceed (in connection to overtraining, etc.) or it may require you to make a revised plan, taking into consideration new information that has come to your knowledge. In our Mount Everest case you could run into weather conditions that would force you to go back to a previous camp and ride out a storm. Or it may require you to make a new route in order to have more favorable weather conditions.

There is no doubt that the better prepared you are the bigger your chances of getting where you want to go.

Now, some of you may say, how about the ability to improvise? If everything is too well planned, don't we risk being too stiff and hang on to our plans for too long? Well the better prepared you are the easier it is to improvise, so if you normally like to wing it but yet want to experience Flow more often, get organized. This is where we start.

Many people when goal setting seem to be preoccupied by what they do not want to happen anymore. If you focus on what you no longer want and you are successful in that pursuit you end up with an open gap and risk going back to the old behavior or that you start doing something equally bad or stupid instead. Let's put this into an example. Let's say you want to stop smoking and you do, but you then leave a gap where you have time on your hands and you need something else to relax you so you start to binge drink instead or start to binge eat. Both of these behaviors are bad for your health, so now you do not die from smoking but from drinking or overeating… not so smart, right?

One more important thing is to consider what you are asking for. You could ask for a red Ferrari but what if you get it and cannot afford driving in it? If you'd rather go for the behavior that can support buying a Ferrari, then you probably also have enough money afterwards to maintain and drive it. So an important suggestion is to go for the behavior that can support what you want to achieve. In this case it would be "making enough money to be able to buy a Ferrari". Makes sense doesn't it?

When creating goals or outcomes, they have to be **Stated in the positive** so that say what you want and not what you don't want. In other words - describe the desired state that you want to be in when you get there.

In the example with smoking the positive outcome could be living a healthy lifestyle (activity that supports the intention of the goal), being able to walk up the stairs in the Empire State Building (or a little less ambitious perhaps) or something that you will be able to do once your old behavior is gone, like tasting the food you eat again, etc.

Many times, I have heard people say to me that they want a promotion. Now this is of course stated in the positive, but the question is if this is something that is **initiated and maintained by individual.** Is this something that is within your own control? If not, how can you make it happen? Probably you can't! So you have to make it so that you are the controlling power in initiating and maintaining the process of getting there.

In terms of getting a promotion, you then have to focus on what will get you to a position where you can be considered for a promotion. This is more likely to be in your control. This may require you to have better results. You may need some additional training or education, etc. All something that you can do.

There is another bonus to this that is worth mentioning. If you are dependent on others for your goals to happen, you may have to wait a long time. By taking charge, you are in the driver's seat and it is your foot on the gas pedal.

In order for your goal to become that unconscious direction you feel you must go in, it is important to translate the goal into a language the brain can understand more fully. As the brain operates in representational systems (Visual, Auditory and Kinesthetic, Gustatory and Olfactory) your goals should be expressed **Sensory Specific.** So what will it look like, sound like and feel like when you are there. Be there fully as if it is really taking place. Notice the finer distinctions of how it looks, sounds and feels.

Sometimes we wish for things to happen and when they finally do, we wish we had never asked for it. Do you know that feeling? Well if you don't that's good and if you do, well, the best we can say about the past is that it is over. Obviously when you have a behavior and you wish to exchange that for a new behavior you have to ask yourself "What was the positive intention of the old behavior?" because all behavior is driven by a positive intention. So that means that the positive elements of the old behavior should be maintained in the new behavior and at the same time you should also check that the new behavior is good for you and the people around you. So when you do an **Ecology check** then ask yourself, is this good for me and the important people in my life (Family or colleagues). How will getting this positively affect and influence my life? Can I maintain the positive intention of the old behavior as I do the new?"

As an example: A person who wants to sail around the world singlehandedly and starts out on this but at the same time wants to be a good father and husband. Well, in the middle of the Pacific Ocean he may not feel so well although his goal is in pursuit because he is away from home. So his value/criteria of being a good father is not possible right now and his wife may feel lonely and frightened by her husband being alone on the big ocean and his kids are crying because they miss daddy and are afraid of losing him. Get the point?

The fifth and final thing you have to do is to make your goal **Testable.** How do you know that you have reached your goal? What specific thing will happen when you reach it? How will others know that you have reached it? What difference will it make in your life or career to reach this? These are important questions and you have to be very specific about this, otherwise you may miss getting there.

Let me give a wonderful example from real life. I was delivering a training and was asked to do an extra evening session for a mixed group of junior and senior high potential managers on goal-setting and so on, which I gladly did. I asked for a volunteer and one of the senior managers raised his arm and I asked him what he wanted to do and he said that he would like to complete the New York City Marathon. In itself a good goal stated in the positive and we went down the list and we finally came to the last question. So I asked him "How do you know that you have reached your goal?" Before he could answer, another senior manager in the audience said out loud in a patronizing voice, "What a stupid question! Everyone knows when he has reached his goal. This is a waste of time!" I was just about to answer him and explain why it was not when the guy with the goal himself said, "No, no the goal is reached when I get the medal over my head". At this point in time I smiled, because in the New York City Marathon this happens somewhat after having crossed the finish line. Because of the vast amount of participants you have to line up in chutes and wait for your medal. I then asked him "Why not the obvious answer your colleague suggested?" and he replied (very wisely), "Well some people can push themselves across the finish line and then they are so exhausted that they drop dead. I am so glad you asked me that question because beforehand I would have said the same, but I realized just now that it is later". I didn't comment on the rude remark, but later the guy came over and apologized and told me that he learned a lot about assumptions from that. So the lesson is, do not assume, be specific and you'll be there.

Exercise - Write down the answers to the questions on the paper you started on in the last exercise. If your plan included sub-goals then start doing the exercise for the overall goal and then proceed and do it again for each sub-goal/milestone.:

> 1. **What do you want? (Stated in the positive and related to activity)**
>
> 2. **Is that initiated and maintained by yourself?: Yes or No**
>
> 3. **Describe how it will look, sound and feel when you get there.**

4. **Is getting this good for you, your family and the important people around you in this context and can you maintain the positive intention of your current behavior?**

5. **How do you know that you have reached your goal? What specific thing will happen when you reach it? How will others know that you have reached it? What difference will it make in your life or career to reach this?**

10 COMPELLING VISIONS FOR YOUR DIRECTIONS

Once you have created that highly motivating Well Formed Outcome or goal, it is now time to create a compelling vision for it. The vision serves as a beacon for you in your pursuit. It is the compelling driver that can help keep you on track and motivate you when things are up hill. The model I will use for this purpose is called Logical Levels and is created by Robert Dilts. It is much more than just a model for creating visions, but here I will use for that sole purpose and guide you through. The Logical Levels describes the six levels of abstraction, which are:

1. Spirituality/Purpose/Vision
2. Identity/Mission
3. Beliefs and Values
4. Skills
5. Behaviors
6. Environment

The Logical Levels can also serve as a tool that secures alignment between your goal and what you do, so the process is not only giving you a beacon to aim your direction at, but also a quality test of your goal.

Most people will find it easier to answer the first three questions and then as we go on, they will find it harder and harder. The reason for this is that the majority of us are very operational in the way we think and act and conscious operations are primarily related to the three first categories. There is no doubt that we all, at an unconscious level, also have representations for the last three categories, but our conscious awareness may not be that present.

A lot of people do not find pleasure in what they do and how they live. One of the reasons for this can be that their operations on the first three categories are not synchronized with the last three categories. In other words, they are in a place, doing things and with a certain skill-set that may not correspond to what they find important, what they believe in and what they see themselves as. If there is this imbalance you will experience Mental Entropy and for that reason not get into Flow.

Obviously, many of you may have chosen to create not just one goal but a series of supporting sub-goals and if you want to be thorough, you need to run this exercise for the overall goal and desired outcomes first and then for each of the sub-goals, ensuring that they are all aligned.

Although the model starts with the first level being that of spirituality or vision (and I will call it that from now on), I recommend that you start at the other end of the model. By doing that you start off with the more obvious and it is my experience that most people find this helpful. If you are very abstract and find it hard to focus on details, you may want to start from the opposite end.

The whole point is to mentally position yourself at the very point in time where it is right before you reach your goal. If we go back to the example with completing New York City Marathon and where his proof was having the medal put over his head, it would be right before he bows his head and receives the medal. This by the way also stresses the importance of knowing exactly what activity or event that will mark out completion of the goal. So go to that very point in time where you are just about to achieve your goal and then notice your **Environment**. Where are you and with whom do you do these behaviors? Notice how it looks, sounds and feels being there. Pay attention to details and really be there. Some of you may see yourself in the picture and if that is the case then dive into the experience so that it becomes as if you were really there and the things are going on around you. This is an associated state and is more in touch with your inner feelings and will help you notice the alignment better.

Now standing there, right before you achieve your desired outcome, notice where you are and with whom. It is time to notice your **Behaviors.** What are you doing right now at that point in time right before it happens?

And in order for you to be able to do this, what **Skills** do you have now? Have you had to develop new skills or mental strategies? Could you have had or developed more skills that would have made it easier or better to get to where you are right now?

In order to be where you are now, right here before achieving your desired outcome there has to be things that are important to you and things that you believe in about doing this activity and achieving this goal. **Values and Beliefs** are the daily behavior drivers and without them nothing would happen. Remember that your thinking structures are driven by your values and beliefs, so all the supporting preferences we talked about will be present to some extent in your process towards your desired outcome. So what beliefs do you have about yourself, about others, about the world in general, in the context of doing this activity and achieving your desired outcome? Do these beliefs support you in fulfilling your role? What is important to you in this context, what do you value - in yourself, others, the world in general. Are these values in alignment with and supporting your efforts?

Some people prefer not to go any further than to the Values and Beliefs stage. The reason for that is that many people start to make things too much set in concrete and do not understand that this is a contextual model and that things change and so should you. I personally cannot stress this enough. Things are not static and so should you of course also not be static!

In our pursuit of a given outcome, when we truly want it we become one with the activity of getting there. This also means that the person who seriously pursues his or her desired outcome will start to identify with the role of getting there. As you can imagine, this identity can quickly become a burden if you think this is who you are and you no longer are in pursuit of the same outcome. We see it from time to time, particular with famous sports people or rock stars. When they stop their career they do not know what to identify with and some of them get lost or try to hold on to the old identity and end up in a personal mess. Understanding that **Identity/Mission** is a contextual here and now thing and can be very powerful in supporting you getting to where you want to be.

So Who are you or what role have you taken on in your pursuit of your desired outcome? When you ask yourself this question the obvious answer to many is myself, and yes of course you are yourself. But thinking about that particular role that you have taken on in order to achieve your goal, who are you then? Make sure to make the Identity sound like something you can truly identify with. It should feel really good saying it out loud! And do not be shy about the name of the Identity. This is only for yourself and not for others. So go for it, be a little extravagant.

The final step is the one that connects you to the outer world. This is where you look at the bigger picture and see what else you become part of once you have achieved your goal. **Spirituality/Purpose/Vision** looking at the larger system (i.e. family, co-workers, people needing your service/product, community, etc.). What is your purpose or the impact you wish to have? What higher community will you become part of?

Let's say that you want to become a national politician (Identity). Then your vision could be "I participate in governing and developing my country" because once you have achieved your goal, then that is what you will do.

Many of our goals (career, family, romance, health, purpose in life, etc.) are based on the requests, desires or expectations of others - parents, spouse, teachers, religious leaders, boss, society. These are not our goals and hence do not have the energy that propels us forward to truly achieve our goals.

When we struggle with our goals, almost always there is some hidden inner conflict that must be resolved. Often we are less than fully alive because of these inner conflicts. The following exercise will assist you in identifying these conflicts and realigning your goal with who you really are.

Think about your goal and answer the same questions for the logical levels as you did above. Notice if there is an alignment between the answers.

For example, you may find that achieving your goal would take time away from being with your spouse and children (assuming this is an important value for you). If this is the case, is there some way to adjust your goal or your strategies/action plan to spend time with your family and still achieve your goal? You may wish to ask those affected by your goal, as they often come up with solutions that you would never think of.

This process will allow you to become aware of the alignment (or lack of it) between your inner self and your goals. As you fine-tune your goals and align them with your inner self, you should find that your goals become clearer, more compelling and more easily achieved.

Exercise 1- part one: Creating a Compelling Vision for your desired Outcome. For every step, write down you answers.

> 1. **Go to that very point in time where you are just about to achieve your goal and then notice your Environment.** Where are you, with whom do you do these behaviors? Notice how it looks and sounds and what feels like being there. Pay attention to details and really be there now.
>
> 2. **Now standing there, right before you achieve your desired outcome, notice where you are and with whom.** It is time to notice your

Behaviors. What are you doing right now at that point in time right before it happens?

3. **In order for you to be able to do what you are doing right now, being here right before you achieve your desired goal, what Skills do you have now?** Have you had to develop new skills or mental strategies? Could you have had or developed more skills that would have made it easier or better to get to where you are right now?

4. **In order to be where you are now, right here before achieving your desired outcome there has to be things that are important (Values) to you and things that you believe (Beliefs) in about doing this activity and achieving this goal.**

5. **So Who are you or what role or Identity have you taken on in your pursuit of your desired outcome?**

6. **Now being where you are, right before you reach your goal, doing what you are doing, having these skills, knowing what's important to you and what you believe in and being who you are, with that identity, this is where you**

look at the bigger picture and see what else you become part of once you have achieved your goal.

What is your purpose or the impact you wish to have? What higher community will you become part of when you have fulfilled your goal? Say it in one short sentence, clear enough so that any kid will be able to understand and repeat inside and adjust it until it feels really good and then write it down.

11 FEEDBACK

Are you making progress yet? This interesting question may seem so obvious and simple and yet many people do not pay enough attention to their feedback systems and this may in turn get them into Mental Entropy and thus prevent them from experiencing Flow. Feedback is deeply related to your thinking structures or Meta Programs if you like. The contextual preference for internal or external source is a factor overlooked by many and in management and sports in particular. How do we learn the best and how do we stimulate ourselves the best?

So let's revisit the Thinking Structures for a moment and dive into the deeper meaning of the category Source for a moment.

A person who becomes motivated by judgments from external sources needs feedback from others in order for them to acknowledge their own progress and success. If they do not get that external feedback they may lose their motivation and even worse become so frustrated that they quit what they are doing. A person who has an External source as their preference will be very open to suggestions from their coaches or managers and as such are easier to help, but as their coach or manager you have to remember to constantly give them this feedback as they otherwise may become demotivated or may be sitting there inactive waiting for your feedback before they go on to the next step.

People who are using their own internal standards do not need external feedback or at least have a very limited need for this! If people with an Internal preference get too much feedback they may react negatively as they find it foolish and/or unnecessary. Because of the internal standards, people who are Internal learn faster due to the fact that they don't have to wait for the feedback from others. Of course this also means that there is a risk of an internal person moving too far in the wrong direction because they themselves think that they are doing great and realize too late that they are not.

Many managers seem to have an Internal preference. This can probably be explained with the fact that because they learn faster and do not have to wait for input from others which in turn allows them to decide faster, they may appear more apt for promotion.

This is an interesting scenario, because if they have an internal preference in their role and context as a manager, they may not fully understand the true need of a person with an External preference for feedback and may thus be giving way too little feedback which in turn will demotivate the person with the need for a lot of External feedback. Or, it may prevent the person from understanding the progress they have made and this can then in turn lead to demotivation.

The above mentioned may send a signal about being Internal is the only thing that works, but this is not the intention and is definitely also not he truth. Internal people can be very stubborn and may therefore have to spend a lot of energy on the wrong things because the advice they got initially didn't meet their own internal standards. The history of the world is full of examples of rulers or other famous people who would only listen to themselves and as such failed in their attempts at their goals or visions.

In reality all people can achieve the wonderful state of Flow and no matter if you have an Internal or an External preference you need some of the other one as well. So, people with an Internal preference need to set up an external system from which they can get input that can keep them on the right track and people with External preference need to establish an internal system on which they can rely for decisions on their own.

If you are one of those who just knows yourself if things are right or wrong or whether you are having success or not you need to establish an external system for feedback that can help you stay on track. Think about people within your context that you trust and respect, people whose opinion you value and make a list of them. What qualities do they possess that make you trust, respect and value them?

Once you have the list complete look at it and notice who could be useful for which kinds of feedback. This way of shortlisting will help you identify who you should set up a feedback system with. Now, as they may also be internal they may not know when you need the feedback or how to give feedback. So, make an agreement with them about the type of feedback you are looking for and how often you need it and get their commitment to giving you this feedback. Be very particular about instructing them about showstoppers – things where they should go "Full STOP" to you ad where they should just offer kind advice.

As people with internal preferences typically do not like getting instructions, unless it matches their standards, you may be prone to objecting their advice. You also have to tell them up front that this may happen and that they should point it out when you object and that they should remind you about the fact that you have asked for it and that you are now not being true to your own standard, which initiated this feedback originally. It may help if they tend to suggest things instead of giving it as commands or instructions, but if they see or hear any predetermined showstoppers, they should use direct and commanding sentences to get you to stop.

I know what I have just suggested may sound really, really weird and to some extent it is, but it will help you and that is what you are looking for, isn't it?

If you need external feedback in order for you to know if you have done a good job or if you can proceed in your learning process or need feedback in order to know if you are successful, then you need to set up an internal system that can help you – particularly in those situations where you cannot get immediate feedback and as a result of that may become frustrated due to the lack of feedback.

I want you to think of a situation where you made a good decision and when you think about it now it is still a good decision. In your mind there will be some kind of visual representation of this experience. Notice where it is placed in your visual field in front of you and notice how far the visual representation is from you.

(It may be worth noting that people's visual representations are very individual and can vary a lot from person to person. Some people's visual representations flash by so fast that they hardly pay any attention to them, so if it doesn't come to you as a steady visual representation when you think about that good decision, you may want to think more about the decision and all the good things that came out of your decision).

Now knowing where the good decision is in your visual field you may also want to pay some attention to the feeling that comes from thinking about that particular decision and where that feeling is located in your body. You may even be able to notice that the feeling is spinning in a certain way inside you. Generally speaking, feelings are either tumbling forwards or backwards or rotating clockwise or counter clockwise.

Now, I want you to think of a decision that when you made the decision seemed like a good decision but when you think back to it now, you know now that it was not a good decision. It may be something you bought and thought you couldn't live without and since then you haven't used it or it may be something completely different. Again notice as you think about it where the location of the visual representation is and where the accompanying feeling is located and if you can, notice also the direction that feeling is spinning in.

My guess is that the pictures are in two different locations. Sometimes very far away from each other and sometimes closer, but not in the same location. My guess is also that the feeling attached is not the same and if you were able to notice the spinning direction even that may not have been the same... right?

Now, I want you to think about something you have to decide soon and where you have not made up your mind yet. Think first about the most likely outcome of your considerations and notice where that visual representation is. My guess is that it will be either in the same place as one of the other ones or at least close by. If there is an alternative you are considering, you may want to try that one out too.

Initially you have to run this process consciously but if you run it enough times, your unconscious will learn to pay attention to these signals and help you make decisions in the future, so that you don't have to wait for feedback. At least not from someone else that is.

Now, just in case that you want to wear both a belt and suspenders, you could ask the people in your context to give you more frequent feedback. That is not going to help you make decisions on your own more easily but it will ensure that you get what you need in order to maintain motivation and avoid frustration. And if you explain why you need it more frequently most people have absolutely no problem giving it to you. Remember, they may have an Internal preference and thus not have the need themselves and therefore not understand your need — without an explanation.

So are you making progress now? You should know and now you do know don't you! And just in case you don't you now have set up a feedback system that will auto generate it for you, haven't you!

12 STAY FOCUSED

One of the things that make the real difference between people who get into Flow and the ones who do not is the ability to stay focused, to concentrate on the activity and not having your mind everywhere else at the same time.

It will be very different as to what generates distraction in people so you have to consider the following; do you generally find it easy to stay focused but are just lacking focus now or do you generally find it hard to keep focus and attention?

If you normally find it quite easy to stay focused but you currently do not, the reason is probably something that is preoccupying your mind in the current moment. This can be many things but must obviously be something you consciously or unconsciously find it necessary to focus on. Here, we are not talking about how useful doing that is for you, but only that somehow you have decided to do it. If you are troubled with a bad memory or something is stuck inside you and you keep thinking about, there's probably (if you pay attention) an image attached to the thought. A very efficient method to get rid of that image is called the SWISH pattern and was developed by Dr. Richard Bandler. It can be done in many different ways, but for this purpose we will use a very fast and simple method and it goes like this:

Look at the image you have that troubles you. Notice the intensity of the internal emotions attached or triggered by looking at this image. Keep looking at the image and then suddenly shrink it down to a 5 inch circle. When you have a nice little round circle then turn it all black NOW and then turn it white NOW and then go black, white, black, white, black, white as fast as you possibly can. Check that it finishes of in all white. Now break the state, so think about something completely different and then go back and look at the 5 inch circle and notice if the feeling is still there. Most often it will be completely gone and sometimes there will be a little bit left, but not in any way disturbing.

Now add to that having the right breathing. One very simple method is just to focus on your breathing and then start taking a deep breath in through your mouth and let it slowly out through your nose and for every breath in, take one in deeper all the way down below your bellybutton. I know it may sound almost too simple but I have found that many people who stress or have too many other things racing around in their mind can be helped a long way with just a little more focus on deep breathing. Apart from forcing their mind to focus on something else than the distracting issue, it also adds more oxygen to the system and the brain, which again is a contributor to better thoughts. At the end of the chapter you will find two more breathing exercises, originally intended for helping people relax, but here used for concentration and ventilation (oxygen supply).

Of course there is nothing as powerful as keeping your goals and dreams present in your mind and life at all times, no other exercise or particular way of breathing can substitute the awareness of where you want to go. You can imagine that if you want to travel to a place you have not been before and there are no road signs or GPS to guide you, then it will be difficult to find your way. We can to some extent compare road signs with milestones, which in fact was part of the original purpose of milestones. Imagine you are the captain of a ship, then you have beacons to guide you and before that you could navigate by the stars. The beacons you set up will help you focus on where you are going and make sure that you do not get astray.

There are many ways of making your milestones or goals visible. You can make posters of them and post them on your bedroom wall or ceiling, you can post them on the door to your fridge, you can create screensavers with them and you can write little notes and put them in between your clothes so that you are constantly reminded visually.

You can also remind yourself by frequently saying them to yourselves. You can tell a lot of people and ask them to remind you, thus creating outside pressure if you have an external reference.

I personally like to visualize them inside my mind, seeing myself reaching each of the milestones or my end goal. I do not associate myself into reaching the goal although it is very tempting. The reason I do not do this is that I do not want the feeling of already having achieved it, risking being satisfied before time, so I prefer to see myself reaching it and then asking myself "Do you want this?" and to no surprise the answer is "YES!".

No matter what, it is profoundly useful to keep your goals in sight – as people often say "Out of sight out of mind" so think about how you can make your goals more visible in all aspects of life!

In the following you will find several exercises that are all designed for helping you to focus and maintain concentration.

Visualization exercise:

Close your eyes and see yourself reaching your goal or one of the milestones. See, hear, feel how it is like when you reach it. Notice what you are doing and notice that you are still on the right track, notice the good feeling you have inside when you see yourself reaching the goal and then ask yourself "Do I want this?"

If you want to make this even more effective find a piece of your favorite music and play that in the background when you do the visualization and then every time you hear the music, you will consciously and unconsciously be reminded about your goal.

You can take this to an even higher level of efficiency by adding not only the music, but also posters around your living space and finally you can attach a word or a sentence when you have the really great feeling in the first part of the exercise and then use this word as a mantra while you are in pursuit.

If you are so lucky that you know someone who is good at practicing NLP, you could also ask them to install these things into your unconscious adding posthypnotic suggestions about what things in your life that will help trigger your mind to remember your goal and remind you about what to do to stay on track.

1) Breathing Exercises:

1. **Sitting, standing or lying down.**

2. **Breathe in and out and count while you do it – same pace – both in and out.**

3. **Practice slowly making the breathing out twice as long as the in.**

4.   **You will experience different sequencing and that is ok… sometimes 2/4 others time 3/6 etc.**

Continue doing this for 10 minutes and add in more times a day

2) Breathing Exercises:

   1.   **Sit comfortably, straight back, parallel lines, hands resting on thighs.**

   2.   **Focus your attention on your breathing and study it without judging it.**

   3.   **Notice if there is a small pause after breathing out before you take the next breath.**

Get to know the pause – quite often it is a quiet space, with no thoughts, where you can find peace

Concentration Exercise - Time Arrow (Leo Angart)

A very important aspect of being able to deal with stress is your ability to focus and not allow other thoughts or things from your environment to interfere. The following exercise can help you do that. The exercise can be done as a floor exercise, or you can have someone doing this to you in a trance, in order to install it even deeper.

Steps:

1. **Relax and imagine your timeline, notice where you have the Past, Present and the Future.**

2. **Place the point of the Present being present right in front of you.**

3. **Put the point of your Past behind you at an 45 degree angle to your left and then put the point of your Future behind you at an 45 degree angle to your right, so that your timeline now has the shape of an arrowhead.**

4. **Step onto the point representing the Present moment and notice the feeling of really being there and then step back half a step and look at the point of the present.**

5. **Hold this attention and anchor it.**

6. **Recall and enhance the anchor any time you need it.**

7. **Now wrap up your timeline and return it to its usual shape and bring it back to this shape whenever you feel like.**

13 SKILLS

In the wake of the coaching tsunami that has washed across the globe the last ten years, it appeared as if all the coaching gurus forgot a very determining factor. They all seem to follow the same mantra, that if you have a goal and the motivation to get there then everything is dandy. I couldn't disagree more.

Knowing where you want to go and wanting to get there is only half of the equation. So many cheerleading motivational speakers can generate that wonderful feeling of internal wellbeing that comes from the wanton motivation yet people have to come back for more and more, because for some strange reason they still don't get to where they want to be although it appears that they have what it takes. So what is missing? Why don't they just go and do it?

At the same time as NLP started, something else happened that also would impact the world in an immortal way. The concept of Situational Leadership was invented by Ken Blanchard and Paul Hersey and the similarities in the way both of these concepts and methods came about are amazing.

Dr. Richards Bandler was the creative student of mathematics and John Grinder was the established linguistic professor when they met. Ken Blanchard started as the teaching assistant for Paul Hersey. In both cases, the combinations of genius minds led to remarkable contributions.

Maybe it is a coincidence, but one of the things that I have learned from being so fortunate to work closely with both methods and the people behind them, is that motivation is only half, and it is nothing without skills and vice versa. Knowing how to do things and having experience is a vital part of being able to do it and getting it done.

Many people have attempted stuff, gotten stuck and lost interest or confidence due to not getting there. If, for example, you want to cross the street. You have tried it once before and went to the side of the street and closed your eyes and then started walking and halfway over the street, you were hit by a car, right, you could say that you were not so successful in reaching your goal. Now in terms of Flow you may have felt great in the process of getting there until you got hit by the truck, but is it not profoundly useful to repeat the attempt? As you really desire the goal of getting to the other side of the street, you then hire a personal coach trained according to the highest standards of international coaching federations, which unfortunately do not include the concept of skills! He or she gets you to focus on your goal, maybe even sharpen your goals and in the best cheerleading traditions, gets you highly motivated to cross the street again. So, full of good intentions you attempt again, this time with even more enthusiasm and wanton desire, so you get to the street, close your eyes and start walking and get hit by a truck.

We need to know how to do things and that is why the modern coaching idea about not helping with building skills is fraudulent because all it guarantees is that you have to get back to the coach, which is why they want to sell you 10 or 20 sessions in one package. If they were really good at helping they ought to be able to help you in one or two sessions. Think about that!

Going back to Situational Leadership and using the approach called Situational Leadership® II by Ken Blanchard (see www.kenblanchard.com for in depth details and information on products and trainings), it looks at two primary components and the balance between those two, which are Competence and Commitment. So in other words CAN you do it and do you WANT AND BELIEVE that you do it. It's a simple formula but maybe that's the reason that it has outlived any other leadership concept, any other leadership method and been spread more globally than any other concept or method, simply because it makes so much sense and as such it is surprising how modern day coaching for a while managed to push competence aside or in some cases almost overboard!

Looking back to the amazing times before the financial crisis that hit the world in 2007 and 2008, maybe there is a connection. Juts maybe too many people attempted to do things only with motivation but lacking the skills. Think about that for a while!

Now obviously you can experience Flow in the process of learning and development and that is for sure a beautiful state. The reason I bring in the concept of skills here is that they are a vital part of your resources. If you want to continue experiencing Flow on the same activity then you constantly have to raise the bar of the challenges and then develop and/or get the necessary skills and or resources.

Those of you reading this book and who work with coaching or managing will know that a common problem seems to be people lacking self-confidence or who have a low self-esteem, although not always. Then quite often these people also lack skills or do not know how to appreciate the skill level they have. So, depending on the issue, we can either direct their attention to the skills level they already have or we can get them to focus on developing their skills.

Most often people have not thought about it in this way and they may suddenly become aware of the skills they need to develop which may also be a mental skill they need. Or they may need to realize and appreciate the skills they already have, which again is a mental process. So, in order to keep experiencing Flow you need to have skills, physical as well as mental skills. Going back to Situational Leadership® II, the dimension called Commitment consists of two elements; Motivation and Confidence and the motivation is of course the want to do it. However, we also have the question of do I believe I can do it. For some strange reason we find many people who have the physical skills but lack the confidence in their own abilities. If that is the case, it would make very much sense to help them build the self-confidence. However, it is important for me to stress that if they do not have the actual skill you are not doing them a favor by building a belief that they have it. Then you should rather focus on the fact that they can get the skill. For some people this can be a showstopper because their self-confidence is so low that they think that they can't do a particular thing or may not even be able to start on it.

If you happen to be one of those people who questions your own abilities, although you have been doing it for a while and ought to be able to do it, you can do the following exercise. If you already have a high degree of self-confidence and you know that you can do it but would like to increase your skills you can go directly to the second exercise. Of course if you are in doubt or want to be even better you may want to do both of them just to be sure, but that is completely up to you.

The vMAX experience

1. **First you have to create your own unique movie theatre.** So sit down and make yourself comfortable. Create a screen 360 degree around you and install a sound system that can give you the most wonderful experience.

2. **Now think of a skill that you have and have exerted for a while but where you feel you lack some confidence.**

3. See yourself performing that skill up on the big screen and notice what you are doing.

4. Now go back to last time you did it and see yourself perform well and then go back to the time before that and see yourself performing well again and once more go back and see yourself again performing well.

5. Now ask yourself "Having seen this again and again what is it that I am missing?

6. Go back to the first experience and then add what may be missing if anything at all and make your visions come closer and bigger.

Notice how much resources you really have now and how little you used it and then run the movie again in 3D and full color where you see yourself utilizing much more of your resources.

7. When you are fully using everything of your skills and resources step into the movie and become one with yourself and your skills and feel how good it feels to know that you have more and that you can use it NOW.

The TUCOR (Turbo Charger on Resources)
by Robert Dilts.

1. Create a timeline on the floor; determine where you have the **Past, Present** and **Future** stored on a line around you.

2. Think of the resource you'd like to enhance.

3. Realize how much (or little) you have of it now and step into the **Present** moment.

4. Now slightly move forward to the future and realize how your resource is growing as much as you need it to.

5. Realize you have the resource as much as you need it at this point, step out of your timeline and take it to the point of the **Present** and feel the difference.

6. Repeat step 4. and 5. Several times.

7. Anchor your powerful resource you just created for yourself (by touching your thumb and index finger or something else that you

quickly can access like saying a word or making a move physically).

8. Step out of your timeline and realize what you will sense for sure coming into a situation where this powerful resource is helpful to you and connect your anchor to that sensation.

9. Wrap up your timeline being sure the resource will be with you anytime you need it.

14 GET THE STATE

As much as we have talked about various techniques and exercises that can help get you into that wonderful state of Flow, you could also design and generate the state yourself. Wouldn't that be something?

Now if you think back to the first steps towards Flow, you have to know where you want to go, so it is crucial that you have your goal out there in front of you in order to set a direction for you. As we have talked about before, your goal should be behavior related so that it can generate things for you, where as if your goal is a thing it may not be sustainable. Knowing what you want in terms of behavior, then this requires you to be in a certain state of mind and why not attempt to be in Flow as much of the time as humanly possible?

Another very crucial skill is smiling. Yes I know, it sounds crazy, but smiling is contributing to build the right chemicals in your brain. With the right chemicals in your brain you can think better and the better you think, the better solutions you can come up with and then you can spend your time pursuing good solutions and feel good about that instead of running around frustrated in a state of Mental Entropy and feeling bad about yourself. Quite simple isn't it? Well maybe so, but many people seem to be unaware of the power and impact of smiling and now, at least you do know, so you can't say I didn't tell you.

Flow typically occurs when people are deeply immersed and engaged in an activity. Let's just say that you would like to be in Flow in the pursuit of your goal, then we could also say that your Desired State is Flow. The question then becomes "Where are you coming from?" in this pursuit. In other words – what is your present state?

Take a seat in your own movie theatre and see a huge big screen in front of you. Make sure that you sit comfortably with both feet on the ground and make sure you breathe in way that makes you relax and feel good. If you don't know how to do this, then breathe in deep with your mouth and slowly exhale out through your nose and keep taking your breath deeper and deeper until you can feel the relaxation spread throughout your body.

Now being fully relaxed see yourself up on that big screen in front of you doing what you are doing now, the present state. Notice how you look and what it sounds like and pay attention to your feelings seeing and hearing yourself and also notice if it is accompanied by any internal dialogue.

Now go to a neutral scene, a place where you don't really care and from there move on to your desired state. So see yourself being in Flow in the pursuit of your goal. Hear yourself and the sounds around you in that state and notice the feeling accompanying seeing and hearing yourself being in that desired state.

I know that there are things that you understand fully and things you believe fully. So first think of a thing that you know you understand and notice what comes to your mind and keep that thought right out there in front of you. Then think about a thing that you believe fully, like the sun will come up tomorrow and place that thought again right in front of you, so that you have both of these on top of each other and can see right through them to the big movie screen in front of you, so that you can fully understand and believe what you have up there on your big screen. Make sure that the understanding and belief frame is as big as the screen or bigger, and if not then adjust NOW!

Knowing now where you want to be and where you are coming from it is time to look at how you will get there. So starting from your Present State, all the way to your Desired State, from how it is to how you want it to be, design the Sequence of Success that will make you achieve your Desired State Conditions. Unfold it step by step, identifying for each step the Values (what's important to you at this point), the Beliefs (what must be true for you at this point in time), your Identity/Identifications (who are you/who do you identify with at this point in time), what Emotions and Mental States will support you at this particular point in time & what Behaviors you should display in order to achieve this step and finally what Resources, Strategies & Skills you need to have in order for you to achieve *Desired State*. *What it is that you really do want!* Draw upon any past successes, similar outcomes or models of excellence who have achieved similar results that you desire.

Once you have made this thorough plan for how to achieve each step and support your way towards your desired state, then from the beginning now, make your first run through the *Sequence of Success* again, as if it were a movie. Go from *Present State to Desired State*, towards making your *Vision of Success come alive on the inside first.*

Obviously it is important to make sure that whatever you do is not hurting other parts of your ecology, so *now*, check if it is "good for you & the ones you love or care about". *Ask yourself:* Is there any part of me that has any objection to me achieving this Desired State or Vision of Success? Is what I've designed okay, acceptable, satisfactory and good enough for me now?

If okay/Satisfactory, then do *Success Conditioning*. Go through the *Sequence of Success* several times on the Mind Screen in front of you from Present State to Desired State, from the beginning to the end. Observe the sequence closely attending to whether it is smooth or pleasing. Take the opportunity, through each run, to identify any "additions or editions" to be made towards your Desired State and your plan to get there.

Add or edit anything you'd like to that will make it even more pleasurable or satisfying to you. If you do make any changes, go ahead & re-run the *Sequence of Success* having made the additions or editions you have targeted or designed.

If there are no additions/editions, then go ahead & bring it off the screen into the middle of your mind, into what we call the "Virtual Reality Zone of the Mind". Then, mentally step into it; fully associate yourself into the situation by looking through your eyes, three dimensionally surrounding yourself with the experience. See what you see, hear what you hear, feel what you feel & do what you do. Run through the entire experience from beginning to end, associating to how it feels & whether or not you believe you can achieve it. **Do it!**

Now, take the "Onlooker or Observer" position in the *back of the mind* (as if you are looking at yourself as the actor in the movie) & envision your timeline from where you are now, (Your Present State), to where you want to be, Desired State (in your future). Then, look forward, out into the future, 1 week, 1 month, 3 months to a year and see these results really happening in your life. **Ask yourself:** Is the effect on my life positive & productive? Is it the way I want it to be? If so, exit & return to neutral, clear your mind, return to normal awakened awareness.

If not okay, go back and make the needed additions/editions that would make it more pleasing & satisfactory. Check it again for Ecology. Keep repeating these steps until you do achieve your Desired State, exactly the way you want it (your Outcome).

Now return to the theatre seat or middle of the mind and access it – step into that premium solution and try it on and then feel the difference. Does it feel good doesn't it? If you like it then return to seeing yourself there and then ask yourself "Do I want this?"

How do you feel now? My guess is pretty good or perhaps even great, because now you know that this will happen, don't you?

This chapter has been based on a technique called "The Desired State Generator" developed by my good friend Elvis Lester, Master Trainer of NLP In Hypnosis You can access an audio version of this exercise online at http://www.execulearn.com/media/DesiredStateGenerator1-1.mp3. Enjoy!

15 THE NOT SO FLOW SCENARIOS

You will come across many people who for some reason are very far from Flow. These people are either stressed from too many challenges and too little resources or they are bored (another kind of stress) and have too many resources and too little challenges.

Getting people back into a balanced situation where they have a chance to experience some kind of wellbeing is a vital skill and with the right guidance, even for these people Flow can occur.

If people are challenged above their skills for longer periods they may very well experience stress. For people with stress, Flow will be impossible to reach and in order to get them back on track several things are required, beginning with giving them back control of their lives and relaxation. A very good tool for that is trance work.

For people who are de-motivated because of too little challenge, they too will be in a condition of stress although not so devastating as the above, it is still having an impact. First of all see if there are chances of finding challenges inside their current task and if not, find out where else they can find a challenge and then build the necessary motivation to pursue Flow on that new task.

Having a balance in your life also seem to be a contributing factor although it also appears that people can experience Flow even under the worst of circumstances. However as the purpose of this book is to help people get easier and more often into Flow, I think it is important as one of the steps towards Flow, to ensure that there is a balance and a harmony in peoples life. I like to call this the ecology check and we have touched upon this before but let's finish of by doing this together and in a structured fashion.

Looking at the goal you are pursuing, see yourself in the process of pursuing it, notice, see, hear, feel where you are and with whom you are. Are these surroundings and these people supporting your process of getting there, are they helping you to get to your goal or are they in any way hindering your route to success? And is there anything that needs to be changed or improved in where you are and who you have around you in order to help you get to your goal faster and having more fun getting there, aren't you.

Knowing where you are and with whom you are I want you now to pay attention to what you are doing, so which behaviors can you see, hear, feel yourself do in the pursuit of getting to your goal? Are these behaviors supporting you in getting there? Are you doing the right things for the right reason?

Knowing now where you are and with whom you are and knowing what you are doing I want you to pay attention to what skills and resources you have at this time of the pursuit of your goal. Do you have the skills and resources that you need? Are there any skills or resources that you do not have yet that you have to acquire? Are there any skills that need to be sharpened or resources that need to be enhanced? Do you know where to get the development of the skills or where to find more of the resources you need?

The first three steps we just covered have a lot to do with the operational aspect of getting you to your goal and assuring you that you do not run into Mental Entropy due to operational issues. So having that in place, let's take a closer look at the more abstract levels of thinking, in order to assure that they also support you getting there.

So knowing where you are and with whom you are and knowing which behaviors you have and what skills and resources you have and which you do not have yet in the pursuit of reaching your goal I want you to think about, what in this context of getting to your goal and having Flow in the process of getting there, that is important to you? What must be there? And in order for that to be important and in order for you to be able to get to goal and experience Flow in the process of getting there, what do you believe in? What must be true about you and this context? Are these values and beliefs that you hold consistent with you goal? Are these Values and beliefs aligned with the skills and resources that you have? Are these values and beliefs aligned with what you do and with whom you do it and where you are doing it?

Now having values and beliefs that are aligned with your goal, having the skills and resources that you need or knowing which skills and resources you need to get or enhance and where to do that, knowing what you are doing and what potentially has to be changed in your behavior and you know where you are and with whom you are and you are sure that this is the right environment for you to be in in the pursuit of your goals, then ask yourself "Who am I in this pursuit of my goal?", "What is my identity when I'm pursuing this particular goal?"

Remember that all this is contextual and changeable, so the identity you take on at one time in one context is only for the here and now and does not transpire into all other contexts or stay the same for the rest of your life. Too many times have we seen people who thought that their identity in one context meant that they could do whatever they wanted in all other contexts without appreciating that the other context had a different set of value, beliefs and rules. Examples has been CEO's of big companies who started to feel invincible due to the power they had inside the company and the power and influence that they had on their immediate surroundings and this reality then morphed into their approach to the laws of their country or international laws.

So in this context of getting to your goal and having Flow in the process of getting there, and being in the right place with the right people, knowing what you are doing and how that influences yourself and others and knowing, understanding and appreciating your skill level and resources, knowing what is important to you and what you believe in, and who you are, I want you to tell me what you will become part of once you have reached your goal? What is the higher purpose of achieving the goal? And is this higher purpose one that you truly desire and that is aligned with your own ecological system or are you prepared to take the consequences of getting there and stepping into this new ecological system with the consequences and impact that may have on you and your loved ones?

The above process is a very useful model for aligning and securing balance, harmony and Flow and avoiding Mental Entropy that stems from not being aligned in what you do and what you really want things to be.

16 THE ART OF FLOW

He was struggling. There were no other words for it. The whole day had he been struggling and his mood was in despair. He thought about quitting but knew that he couldn't no matter how much he wanted to. Quitting was not an option, but then what was?

His thoughts were interrupted by the radio in his ear. He heard his sports director's familiar voice "Hang in there, only an hour to go and I know you don't want to lose too much time, do you?"

He replied that his legs felt like concrete and this only one day after his almost legendary victory. There sure wasn't much between being champ and chump.

"Well since you are down here at this end with me you might as well make yourself useful." his sports director said in the radio.

"Drop down to our car and get some water for the other guys."

He grimaced. He knew what that meant. He was now considered expendable so he might as well use his last juice in his body to get water and then just fall all the way back after this one last effort. He had no choice so he dropped back a little further and started to see the different team cars pass by. He knew by the ranking of the teams that he should fall back to car number five so after the first four he looked to his right and there was his sports director with a big grin on his sunburned face.

You could tell that this was a man with many years on the road and in the saddle behind him. That special look in his face and around his eyes that revealed thousands of hours in all weather conditions and training year in and year out, with the sun making its signature on his skin and carving in wrinkles in his face.

"So are we having a bad day at the office or what." He laughed.

"I thought you were going to win another stage for us today. Did you get tired of holding press conferences or did your wife get upset because the beautiful girls on the podium kissed you so much after your victory yesterday?"

He felt like punching his sports director but instead he started to laugh. This was insane. He was almost on the brink of dropping out of the race, he wanted to quit and all his sports director could think about was joking. He laughed even more. His legs screaming for mercy but yet he laughed.

"I wonder if you can remember what goal you set at the start of the season?"

Again his thoughts were disrupted by his sports director.

"I wonder if you can remember what your dream was that day that we talked about it right after New Year's!"

He thought about it for a moment. Here he was, using his last power to get some water and he was then asked if he could remember some stupid thing from seven months ago. Insanity had invaded his team, he thought.

"You are not answering my question." This time the voice was more direct, but still friendly but a lot firmer.

"Well if it makes you happy, the answer is yes I can!"

"I wanted to win a stage in the Tour de France and help my team succeed overall."

"Good boy, so how about focusing a little bit on the second part of your dream and goal?"

"Yesterday everybody rode their sorry butts off in order to help you get the win and today, just because you are not up there with a camera in your face, you want to give up. You want to quit, don't you?" "What do you think could make you an even bigger star in the minds of your fellow teammates and in the eyes of the millions of people watching you right now? Take a wild guess."

He was just about to say that he was already totally forgotten but something prevented him. He looked over his left shoulder and realized that his unconscious had saved him from making an embarrassing statement.

Right there, only a few meters behind him was one of the motorcycles with a cameraman sitting on the back. Having sat there already for two weeks the riders and the TV crews by now knew each other quite well and he immediately recognized the cameraman from yesterday. It was the one who had been in front of him on the last five kilometers towards the finish line. He forced a smile and waived and shouted to the cameraman "Just down here checking on you. Didn't want to ride to the top without you."

He laughed and it felt so good, and he noticed that the cameraman laughed too. Actually the cameraman laughed so much that the camera was bouncing up and down, which only made him laugh even more. He looked into the car of his sports director and both him and the mechanic in there was laughing aloud.

"That's the spirit" his sports director said. "Now how about that second part of your goal?"

"Isn't it about time to do something about that?"

He nodded and for some strange reason his legs already felt a little better, but even more important – his head wasn't hurting any more.

"So what is your plan right now?"

"How do you plan to make sure that the second part of your goal will happen?"

Before he could answer he was interrupted again with a new question from his sports director.

"What state are you in right now and what state would you like to be in?"

"I want to be in a state where I enjoy what I do and I do my best with the resources I have."

Having said that he knew what he had to do so he focused on the present moment and pushed all things from yesterday behind him to his left and all about tomorrow he pushed back to his right and focused on the moment right in front of him and he dived right into that moment and it all became so clear.

He quickly calculated the distance to the finish line. He knew the route and he knew each bend in the road and every little bump on the road. He knew how far he had to ride with a higher cadence in order to catch up with his teammates and supply them with water. He knew who was between him and his team's leading rider. He knew that his best friend and training partner was up there, fighting hard to win, needing the supplies, needing the water and a gel with some fast acting carbohydrates. He knew that he could make a difference and that now it wasn't about him but it was about the team, it was his friend, it was about sacrifice!

He loaded his bike with water bottles and stuffed some more under his shirt so he almost looked like the Michelin man. He started running his favorite internal movie in which he was the team guy who gave it all for his teammates and sacrificed everything he had and the team would win.

He could feel a change on the inside. This wasn't just the good chemicals that came from laughing, this was more, this was the feeling of determination, this was the sense of purpose in life, this was life in itself, this was him and nothing less.

As he had done so many times in practice he started flashing his values in front of him on his internal screen and he started his internal mental body scanner, scanning through his whole body in order to monitor each and every little cell in his body, each and every joint and each and every muscle. He found the place in his body where he could feel that there was still energy, where there was still resources and he started spinning that good feeling round and around in increasingly bigger circles, orbiting around spreading it to more and more of his body and the more he did it the better he felt, the more convinced he felt and he transferred all his resources into his legs and started pedaling with a determined stride, pushing his cadence.

Gradually he started building speed and he noticed how he passed the service cars in front and how amazingly quickly he got up to the rear of the peleton. He heard the motorcycle behind him and automatically put his arm out and raised his thumb. He didn't lose as much as a stride with this gesture but just felt even more power coming back to his legs as he kept running that internal movie seeing himself reaching his teammates in front, giving him the water bottle that would mean the difference between all or nothing.

He passed more and more riders and although he was totally focused and kept looking straight ahead, he couldn't miss their looks of total amazement, seeing him coming back like this, on this part of the mountain. For every rider he passed, he felt even more power and commitment and he went even deeper into himself. He passed a teammate and gave him a bottle and continued as if he hadn't even noticed that he gave that bottle.

He scanned constantly from the tip of his toes all the way up through his legs, his breathing, his heart rate, his pulse, his watt output, his cadence his mouth and back down to the toes and up again.

He felt better and better and he passed more and more riders as their power gave in and the mountain won the fierce fight that every rider was battling against it. He now realized that he was getting close to his teammate, his friend who was up in the front, and it gave him even more energy. He pushed his legs with a fierce force as if he was almost possessed and the world around him disappeared and time stood still and although the landscape passed his view, he felt as if he could fly, as if he was invincible. Sounds stopped and he was in his own little cocoon just flying up the mountain.

His eyes caught sight of a familiar riding style and jersey and his arm went over his shoulder and picked another bottle out from the back of his own jersey. He extended his arm and handed the bottle to his friend, his compadre, his roommate and he saw the look of appreciation, the look of gratitude, the look of witnessing the unbelievable and that look from this person was all he needed, all he wanted and it gave him so much more than anything else.

He handed one more bottle to his friend and then he started pushing his pedals even more and placed himself right there in front of his friend, guarding him from the wind, saving his friend those extra percentages that would mean everything on the last meters of this excruciating stage.

He pushed his legs as hard as he could, sensing that his friend was still holding on to his rear wheel. They had practiced this for a long time, even back to the time when they both had started cycling for real, with a dream of doing just this on the final part of a Tour de France mountain stage. They had taken turns to be the winner. Who would launch off and get the stage win? Sometimes they had sprinted and allowed the best man of the day to have the win. But this was no time for play and yet it felt like he was playing. He felt like he was eighteen and the world was at his feet and nothing but unexploited possibilities. He flashed memories of the hard winter training of the things he had had to miss out on and he praised the good spirits for giving him the mental strength to control himself and his ability to deliver when it really mattered.

He sensed cameras in his face, he sensed the cheering from the crowd on the roadside but he heard nothing, just his own voice shouting "You can show them." over and over again. He sensed a sound in his ear from the radio but paid no attention to it. He knew that he was pushing over his perceived limits but he felt reserves of resources and he could taste his whole body as the taste and smell of hard work spread in his mouth.

He kept monitoring his rear wheel, making sure that his friend was still there and when he scanned his body again he found every little tiny depot of resource and started spinning that into his body, feeding every little fiber with the rest of what was in there. He saw pictures of his wife, his children, his family, his friends, each and every one who mattered to him and he felt good. He felt like he was just floating in the sky, like he was a bird or a feather and although there now was a sense of cramps in his legs he converted the pain into even more determination and he travelled deeper into his own world, hardly noticing the road, hardly noticing the bicycle, hardly noticing being there. It was as if he was floating out of his body, like he was in a trance and couldn't come out, like he was not there anymore.

And all of a sudden everything changed, he was stunned, he was chocked, how could it be, how was this possible, was he dreaming, was he hallucinating, was he dead? Right there in front of him he saw the turn that he knew so well. The final turn on the climb, the turn that was so close to the finish line that there hardly was any room for a sprint. He couldn't believe it, what had happened. He suddenly had a desperate feeling. Had he abandoned his friend? Had he failed to give back what he owed him from yesterday?

He quickly looked around him and saw the tormented face of his best friend forcing a smile on his face. He looked around and realized that together they had simply outraced all the other riders. He couldn't believe it. How had he gotten there? Where did all this endurance come from?

As they came out of the turn he saw the finish line, the distance so short he could almost roll over it without any more pedaling. He looked over his shoulder, his friends face showing pain and agony, his eyes displaying an almost empty look.

"Take it!" he heard his friend whisper. "Do it!"

But he couldn't. His whole system trembled and he pulled the brake so that his bike almost came to a complete stand still and his friend rolled past him with just a few inches to the finish line. It was the biggest moment in his life, better than the day before. This was indeed the euphoric moment that would be with him forever.

As he crossed the line himself, his body gave in, he fell and hit the asphalt with a smile on his lips, feet still stuck in the pedals and the bike following his feet and legs. He started laughing, at first just a little and then more and more until his laughter rung out in between the mountains. It may have sounded like the laughter of a man who had lost his marbles, his wits, his sanity, but it was indeed a man who had conquered himself, who forever after would walk and stand tall. A man who would never look back but would tell the world with pride how time stood still and how Flow showered him in his pursuit of the optimal experience.

ABOUT THE AUTHOR

Anders Piper, Denmark, has an extensive training and performance background working with some of the leading companies in the world, where he has worked globally with Search & Selection, Leadership Development, Communication Training, Coaching, Management, Conflict Management and Mediation.

Anders has worked the last 15 years with Behavior Enhancing Techniques and he holds a Masters of Science degree in Psychology and a degree in Human Resource Development. He is a Licensed NLP Master Trainer from Society of NLP and certified Coach from NLP University. Anders is also certified Identity Compass® trainer, LAB Profile trainer, WealthyMind Trainer and Master Trainer of Situational Leadership® II.

Anders has conducted several workshops on Flow and helped people around the world in the pursuit of their goals.

RESOURCES:

You can find more information about the various people mentioned in this book on the following websites:

Anders Piper	www.come4learning.com
Richard Bandler	www.richardbandler.com
Mihaly Csikszentmihalyi	www.cgu.edu/pages/4751.asp
Elvis Lester	www.execulearn.com
Shelle Rose Charvet	www.successtrategies.com
Identity Compass	www.identitycompass.com
Robert Dilts	www.nlpu.com
Ken Blanchard	www.kenblanchard.com
Bruce Lipton	www.brucelipton.com

Cover photo by photographer Tim De Waele, www.TDWsport.com

For all enquiries about trainings and seminars in
Shortcut to Flow please contact:
Anders Piper
come4learning
Denmark
Website: www.come4learning.com
E-Mail: info@come4learning.com

For information on NLP trainings in your own country
and around the world, go to:
www.PureNLP.com
or
www.nlpinstitutes.com

BIBLIOGRAPHY

Books referred to in this book:

Bandler, R. (1985). *Using Your Brain For A Change*

Blanchard, K (1999). *Leadership and the One Minute Manager*

Charvet, S.R. (1995). *Words That Change Minds*

Csikszentmihalyi, M. (1990). *Flow: The psychology of optimal experience*

Dilts, R. (2003). *From Coach to Awakener*

Dilts, R. (1995). *Strategies of Genius, Volume One*

Lipton, B. (2005). *The Biology of Beliefs*

Other suggested readings:

Bandler, R. (2008). *Get The Life You Want*

Bandler, R. (2008). *Richard Bandler's Guide to Trance-formation*

Anders Piper

Made in the USA
San Bernardino, CA
01 February 2014